W9-BBC-803

## FEARLESS WITH FABRIC

# Fresh Quilts

## FROM TRADITIONAL BLOCKS

### An Inspiring Guide to Making 14 Quilt Projects

**Sarah J. Maxwell**

*Fearless with Fabric Fresh Quilts from Traditional Blocks*

Landauer Publishing (***www.landauerpub.com***) is an imprint of
Fox Chapel Publishing Company, Inc.

Copyright © 2020 by Sarah J. Maxwell and Fox Chapel Publishing
Company, Inc., 903 Square Street, Mount Joy, PA 17552.

Project Team:
Editors: Laurel Albright/Sue Voegtlin
Copy Editor:Katie Ocasio
Technical Editor: Ruby I. Young
Designer: Laurel Albright
Photographer: Sue Voegtlin

ISBN: 978-1-947163-23-2

All rights reserved. No part of this book may be reproduced, stored
in a retrieval system, or transmitted in any form or by any means,
electronic, mechanical, photocopying, recording, or otherwise, without
the prior written permission of Fox Chapel Publishing, except for
the inclusion of brief quotations in an acknowledged review and the
enlargement of the template patterns in this book for personal use
only. The patterns themselves, however, are not to be duplicated for
resale or distribution under any circumstances. Any such copying is a
violation of copyright law.

Note to Professional Copy Services:
The publisher grants you permission to make up to ten copies for any
purchaser of this book who states the copies are for personal use.

The Cataloging-in-Publication Data is on file with the
Library of Congress.

We are always looking for talented authors. To submit an idea,
please send a brief inquiry to acquisitions@foxchapelpublishing.com.

Printed in Singapore

22 21 20    2 4 6 8 10 9 7 5 3 1

This book has been published with the intent to provide accurate and
authoritative information in regard to the subject matter within. While
every precaution has been taken in the preparation of this book, the
author and publisher expressly disclaim any responsibility for any
errors, omissions, or adverse effects arising from the use or application
of the information contained herein.

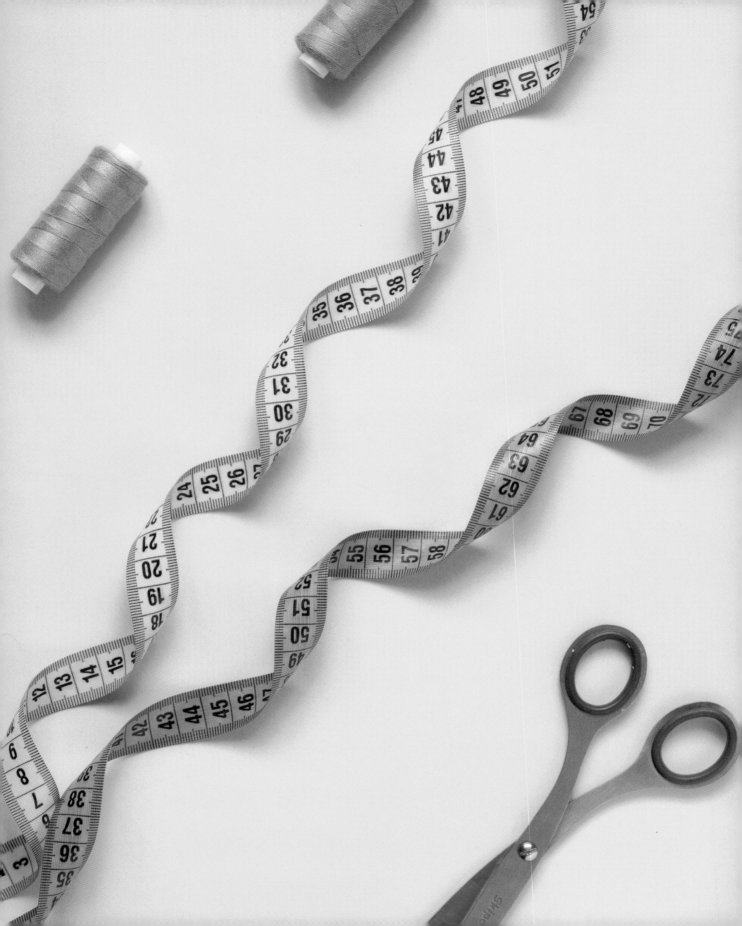

# CONTENTS

# INTRODUCTION

Regardless of experience level, quilters struggle with how to use fabric successfully in quilt design—whether it's color choice or individual fabric placement within blocks. I revel in pairing unusual combinations, manipulating traditional blocks, and doing the unexpected. Helping others to develop confidence, to embrace their own sense of style, to be "fearless with fabric" is a life-long passion.

To me, the play between fabrics and their colors—every shade, hue, tint, and tone, from solid to texture to multicolor print—is the best part of the quilt process.

In the last few years, two additional challenges have emerged—how to make traditional blocks and designs look fresh and new and how to use "modern" fabrics in quilt projects.

Long-time quilters feel that the industry has left them behind as it has embraced modern quilting concepts. Like so many others, I have struggle with how to use "modern" fabrics and how to make quilts my children will love.

*Fearless with Fabric Fresh Quilts from Traditional Block*s will help quilters be confident in their choices and find the courage to use today's fabrics and styles. With a focus on how to incorporate negative space in designs and how to manipulate traditional blocks into modern settings, quilters will develop skills they can apply to future projects.

Each pattern focuses on experimenting with some aspect of quilt design or fabric usage, and provides easy-to-understand guidelines for stepping outside your comfort zone.

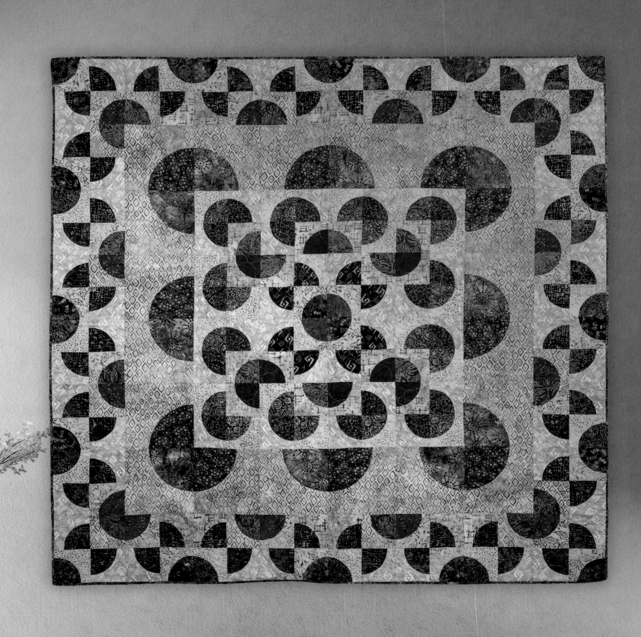

# GETTING STARTED

Whether you are a new quilter or you have stitched for years, the same issues are likely stifling your creativity.

The list to the right contains just some of the questions I hear quilters debate on social media and in quilt shops everywhere. Often we are conditioned to be afraid of trying something new. Whether from fear that someone will criticize our work or fear of investing in materials we aren't sure how to use, a lack of confidence holds quilters back from expressing their own style.

## QUESTIONS I HEAR FREQUENTLY

- How do I make something that looks fresh and contemporary?

- How can I make a quilt that doesn't look just like all the quilts I've already made?

- How do I know these fabrics go together without buying a bundle or a precut pack?

- Can I mix styles of fabric? Can batiks really work with prints?

- Can I mix wovens and textures with cottons in a quilt?

- Do I always need to use a solid for a background to make a "modern" quilt?

- What is negative space, and how do I add it to my quilt?

## You can be FEARLESS WITH FABRIC.

Through a series of quilt projects that explore different aspects of pushing traditional quilt boundaries, I'll explain my approach to design and show you how to have success.

Each pattern focuses on experimenting with some aspect of quilt design or fabric usage, and provides easy-to-understand guidelines for stepping outside your comfort zone.

Look for "Leap of Faith" motivators with some patterns that will give you a concrete suggestion about how to conquer a possible fear.

For even more motivation, refer to the "Confidence Boosters." These tips address common concerns about each technique, from possible construction challenges to adapting different palettes to the project.

Various patterns also include alternative colorways of the design, so you can visualize how the quilt will look using different palettes.

Finally, some patterns include with "Fearless Takeaways"—main concepts that you can apply to future projects.

# Ready to get started?
# LET'S BE FEARLESS!

# COLOR WORM

Staggered rectangles create a repetitive row design, but adding a textured woven background instantly updates this to a more modern look, and expands opportunities to add texture through quilting.

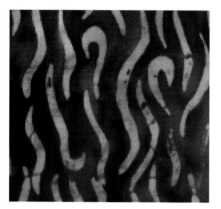

With Color Worm, I combined several elements for a modern take on a simple block. A batik with reds, oranges and purples to define the color story for the quilt.

Next, I selected a woven linen-cotton fabric for the background. Woven fabrics add interesting texture to a quilt. While they are often a bit heavier than regular cotton prints, they are easy to include in a quilt.

This quilt features (40) 9" (22.86cm) finished-block set together in horizontal rows of 8 blocks, alternating with strips of plain background fabric.

## MODERN

The gently curving S-shape created by the staggered placement of colorful strips reminded me of a determined worm, pulling itself along, up and down, a little at a time. The open areas of background are perfect for intricate quilting. With Color Worm, I combined three elements for a modern take on a simple block. First, I selected both cotton prints and batiks for the color elements in the block. Let go of the idea that batiks only play well with other batiks. Their vibrant colors and subtle shifts in value add unexpected sparks to a quilt with no added effort.

By including open areas without piecing, the pieced elements stand out more, and the visual appeal of the quilt is less busy and more relaxing. As an added bonus, with fewer blocks to piece, you can concentrate on adding some great quilting designs or stitchery to the open background areas.

## TRADITIONAL

Without the added background areas, a more traditional quilt would have rows of blocks, side by side like this.

## LEAP OF FAITH

- If you have worked in the same color palette for several quilts, this is the perfect project to try something new. Simple blocks and a limited number of fabrics mean you can step out of your comfort zone and experiment without worry.

## COLOR LESSON

- This is the perfect quilt to experiment with selecting one color as your focus color, and then selecting companion fabrics in shades to the right and left of that color on a color wheel to add accents. In my quilt, red is my focal color. Using a basic 12-step color wheel, I can see that adjacent colors are pink ranging to purple and orange ranging to yellow.

## MATERIALS

- ½ yard (45.72cm) each of 9 assorted prints and batiks
- 6 yards (548.64cm) neutral background print
- 5 yards (457.2cm) backing

## CUTTING

*Keep fabric cuts organized by color and size*

**From the 9 prints, select one print to start each row of color in a block. It will be print "A"**

**From A print, cut:**
(40) 1½" x 5½" (2.54 x 13.97cm) strips

**From each of the remaining 8 prints, cut:**
(40) 1½" x 5" (2.54 x 12.7cm) G strips

**From the background fabric, cut:**
(1)  WOF x 72" (182.88cm). From the piece, cut:
     (4) 9½" x 72" (24.13x 182.88cm) length of fabric strips.
(80) 1½" (3.8cm) B squares
(80) 1½" x 2" (3.81 x 5.08cm) C rectangles
(120) 1½" x 2½" (3.81 x 6.35cm) D rectangles
(120) 1½" x 3" (3.81 x 7.62cm) E rectangles
(40) 1½" x 1" (3.8 x 2.54 cm) F rectangles
(80) 1½" x 4½" (3.8 x 11.42cm) H rectangles
(80) 1½" x 4" (3.8 x 10.16cm) I rectangles
(80) 1½" x 3½" (3.81 x 8.89cm) J rectangles
(10) 2½" x 42" (6.35 x 106.68cm) strips for binding

## QUILT TOP ASSEMBLY

1. Lay out a block to check color placement. Your goal is a smooth transition of color, perhaps from orange to purple or light to dark within a single color family. Step back to check the layout or take a photo with your camera or phone. If you like the placement, start sewing!

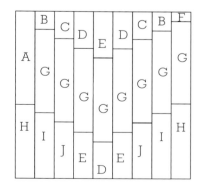

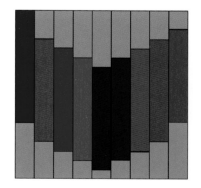

2. Referring to the diagram below, sew background rectangles to each print rectangle. Press the seams toward the dark print. Sew the pieced strips into a block, pressing the seams toward the right. Make (40) blocks. The blocks should measure 9½" (24.13cm) unfinished.

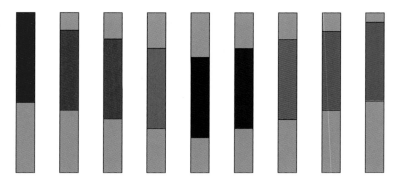

3. Sew the pieced strips into a block, pressing the seams toward the right. Make (40) blocks. The blocks should measure 9½" (24.13cm) unfinished.

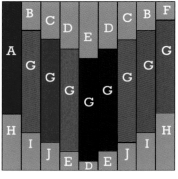

**Make 40**

4. Lay out 8 blocks to create a row and sew. Make (5) rows.

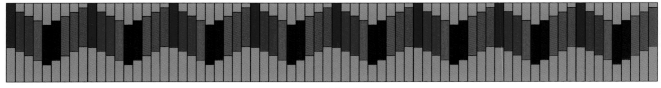

**Make 5**

## FEARLESS TAKEAWAYS

- This quilt would also look great with a dark background and lighter fabrics for the "worm" that dances across the top.

- Add a new fabric type to your usual selections.

- Audition your selections in a test block so you can make any necessary cutting or machine adjustments before continuing with the whole quilt. A test block will also allow you to see how your fabrics play together before you commit to the entire project.

## CONFIDENCE BOOSTER

- If you're unsure about working with a new color or a new fabric type, purchase a few at quarters first and sew a single block. Without the financial commitment of yards of fabric, you'll feel more open to experimenting.

5. Sew the rows together, alternating with a background strip and following the quilt assembly diagram. The quilt top should measure 72½" x 81½" (184.15 x 207.01cm).

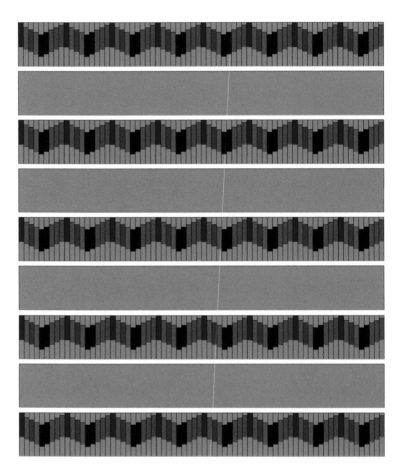

## FINISHING THE QUILT

1. Layer the backing, batting and quilt top, and quilt as desired.

2. Trim the selvedge from each of the binding strips. Sew together using diagonal seams to make one long strip. Press the seams open. Fold the binding in half, wrong sides together, and press along the entire length of the strip. Attach the binding using your preferred method.

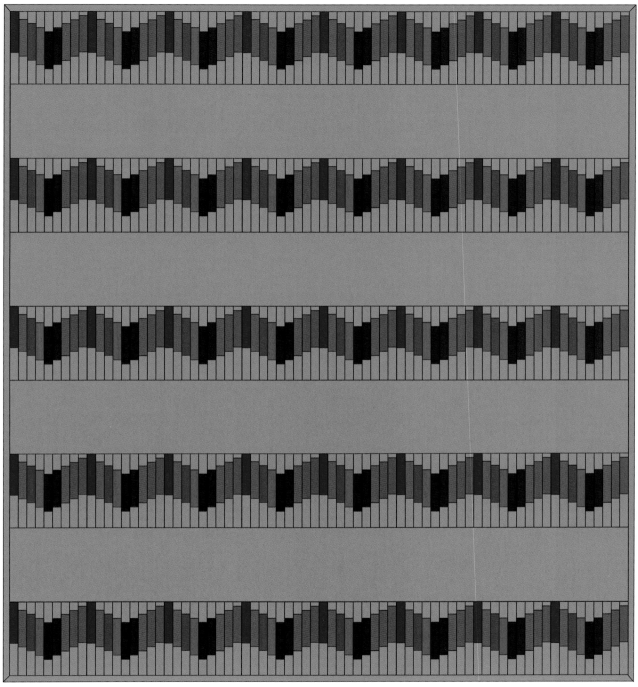

**COLOR WORM**
Finished size: 74" x 83" (187.96 x 210.82cm)

# GIRL'S BEST FRIEND

Traditional one block quilts have always fascinated me, but simply repeating a shape over and over in a limited fabric combination can quickly become boring.

As I played around with various shapes in a computer design program, I realized that working with three sizes of the same shape would greatly expand the design opportunities. The three sizes of diamonds come together to create a scrappy masterpiece.

## MODERN

The evolution of low volume, modern backgrounds—small-scale color or neutral motifs on whites to off-whites to grays—has created a whole genre of scrappy quilt. Combine this feature with a modernized one-patch motif and the design possibilities are endless.

## TRADITIONAL

For years, traditional quilters have loved using their scraps and stash to create one-patch quilts such as postage stamp or hexagon projects.

## LEAP OF FAITH

- Because this quilt uses so many fabrics and is dependent on color and value, consider cutting only part of your fabrics initially. Then build the quilt from the top left corner downward on a design wall, cutting more as the design emerges.

## COLOR LESSON

- Using subtle variations in value and print would add a lot of interest to a quilt.

## MATERIALS

- Large assortment of low-volume backgrounds; fat eighths (9" x 22" [22.86 x 55.88cm]) work well. I started with about 4 yards (365.76cm) and added variety as needed.
- Assortment of prints in 3 colors; fat sixteenths (9" x 11" [22.86 x 27.94cm]) work well. I started with about 24 fat sixteenths each of bright pinks, purples and blues.
- 9 yards (822.96cm) for backing
- ¾ yard (68.58cm) for binding

WOF = width of fabric

## CUTTING

*Keep your cuts organized by size and color to make the block and quilt assembly easier.*

**From the low-volume prints, cut:**
(270) Medium Piece B diamonds.

**From the bright pink prints, cut:**
(42) Medium Piece B diamonds
(4) Large Piece C diamonds

**From the purple prints, cut:**
(14) Medium Piece B diamonds
(4) Large Piece C diamonds

**From the blue prints, cut:**
(10) Medium Piece B diamonds
(3) Large Piece C diamonds

**From the dark gray print, cut:**
(10) 2½" (3.81cm) x WOF strips for binding

## CUTTING THE DIAMONDS

*Note: only half of each cut diamond will be used in the quilt top. Use half-diamonds with a ¼ " (3.18cm) seam allowance. Discard or save leftover pieces for scraps to be used on a future project.*

1. Cut (27) low-volume diamonds in half horizontally. Use the alignment dots on the template, and mark the seam intersection points on the sides of the shape.

2. Align the ¼" (0.64cm) mark on the ruler with the alignment dots. Using a rotary cutter, cut the diamond shapes to create horizontal half-diamonds for use on the top and bottom edge of the quilt. Discard or set aside the leftover parts of the diamonds for another project.

3. Cut (22) low-volume diamonds in half vertically. Use the alignment dots on the template, and mark the seam intersection points on the sides of the shape.

4. Align the ¼" (0.64cm) mark on the ruler with the alignment dots. Cut the diamond shapes to create vertical half-diamonds for use on the side edges of the quilt. Discard or set aside the leftover parts of the diamonds for another project.

5. Cut (4) low-volume diamonds in half, both vertically and horizontally (see steps 1–4), for use in the corners of the quilt top.

## PURPLE PRINT DIAMONDS

Cut (4) Medium Piece B purple print diamonds in half horizontally, following steps 1–2, for diamonds along the top edge of the quilt.

## BLUE PRINT DIAMONDS

1. Cut (3) Medium Piece B blue print diamonds in half horizontally, following steps 1–2, for diamonds along the bottom edge of the quilt.

2. Cut (2) Large Piece C blueprint diamonds in half vertically, following steps 3–4, to use along the side of the quilt top.

## FEARLESS TAKEAWAYS

- Update a traditional one block design by adding variations of the shape in different sizes.

- Rather than using a traditional repeating color plan, vary fabric and value placement to create an offset, more random design.

## CONFIDENCE BOOSTERS

- Consider piecing some of the smaller four-block diamond units into the medium diamond size to speed up quilt construction. Mix and match sets of (4) small diamonds randomly to create "medium diamonds," which can be more easily moved around on a design wall.

- Evaluate larger scale prints on white with an eye toward how they might appear cut up. This is a great quilt to use up those "ugly" or leftover fabrics because they will be cut up into small units where the color takes center stage.

## PIECING THE QUILT TOP

Referring to the Quilt Assembly Diagram, lay out diamonds. Start in the upper left hand corner and piece the quilt in diagonal rows. Sew the rows together to finish the quilt top.

## FINISHING THE QUILT

1. Layer the backing, batting and quilt top. Quilt as desired.

2. Trim the selvedge from each of the binding strips. Sew together using diagonal seams to make one long strip. Press the seams open. Fold the binding in half, wrong sides together, and press along the entire length of the strip. Attach the binding using your preferred method.

## ALTERNATIVE COLORWAY

Quilt Assembly Diagram

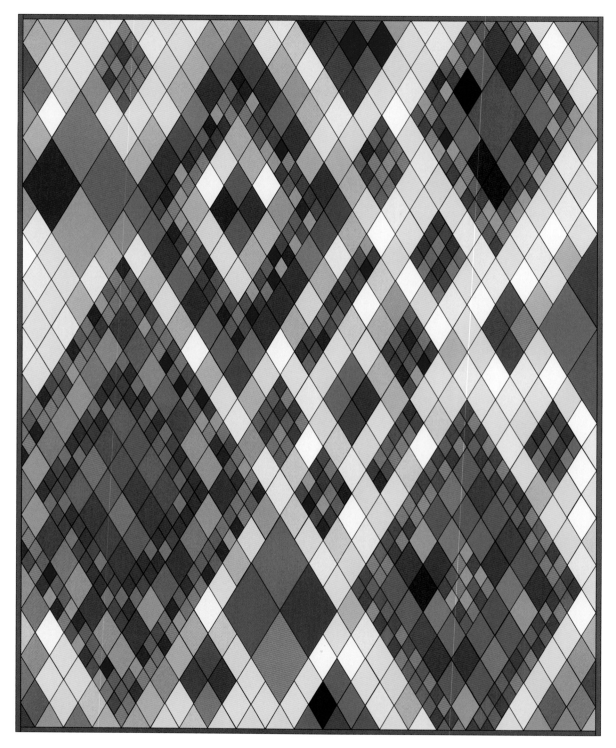

**GIRL'S BEST FRIEND**
Finished size: 82" x 106" (208.28 x 269.24cm)

# Girl's Best Friend Templates

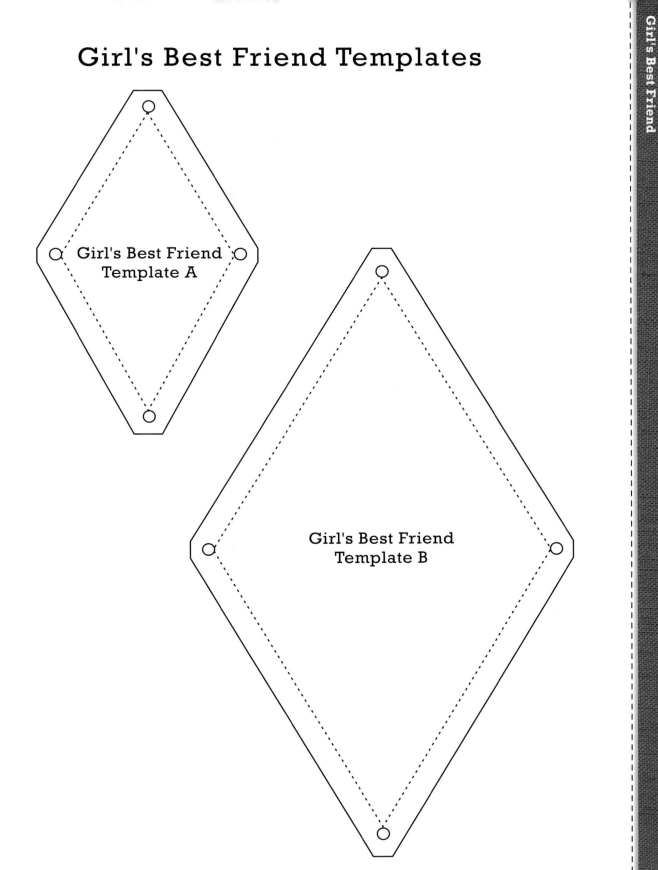

Girl's Best Friend
Template A

Girl's Best Friend
Template B

# Girl's Best Friend Templates

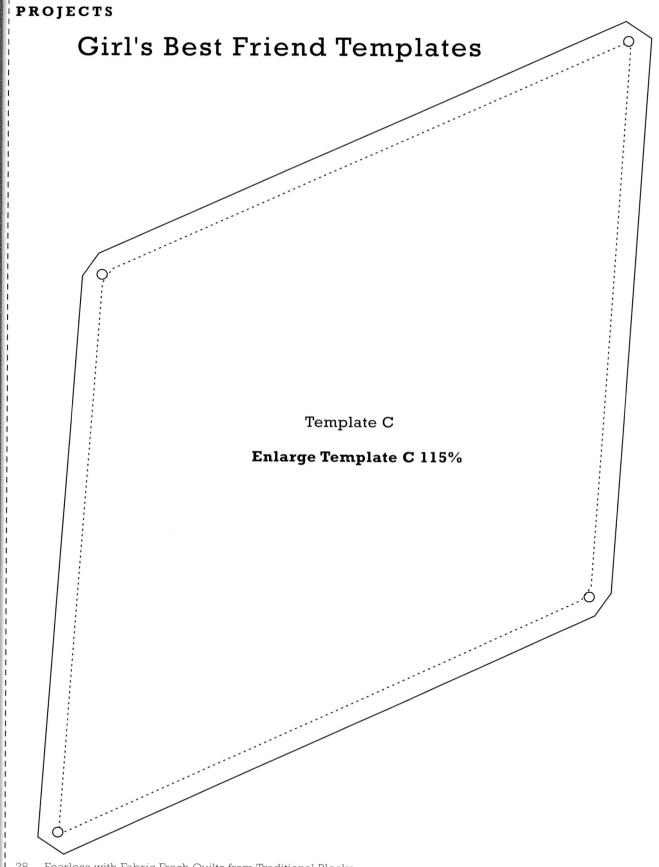

Template C

**Enlarge Template C 115%**

# LEFT OF CENTER

Left of Center evolved from my interest in playing with scale and wanting to showcase the bubble print in large pieces.

Placing a nine-patch element in the center plain square adds another design element, and allows a couple of other fabrics to be included.

## MODERN

Surrounding simple nine-patch units with sawtooth frames, and then positioning the main block elements in a corner of the quilt rather than in the center, left lots of negative space to showcase quilting designs.

By using a large-scale and off-center set, a single block becomes the focus of the entire quilt.

## TRADITIONAL

This concept started off with the traditional Sawtooth Squares block. When set traditionally in a small size, the block is a piecing challenge.

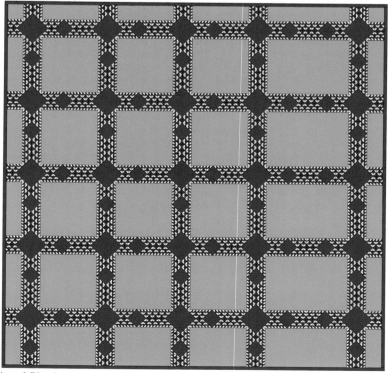

## LEAP OF FAITH

- Any traditional block is a candidate to be significantly enlarged to represent the entire quilt design. To add interest, include a pieced frame or border.

## BLOCK SIZES

Half-square triangle block: 3½" (8.89cm) unfinished

Blocks 1A and 1B: 15½" x 18½" (39.37 x 46.99cm)

Blocks 2A and 2B: 18¾" (46.99cm)

Blocks 3A and 3B: 18½" x 21½" (46.99 x 54.61cm)

## YARDAGE REQUIREMENTS

- ⅜ yard (34.29cm) green print/solid
- ⅜ yard (34.29cm) blue print/solid
- ½ yard (45.72cm) light purple print/solid
- ½ yard (45.72cm) dark purple print/solid
- 4½ yards (411.48cm) white print/solid
- ¾ yard (68.58cm) white print/solid for binding
- 4½ yards (411.48cm) for backing

## CUTTING

*Keep your cuts organized by size and color to make the block and quilt assembly easier.*

**From the green fabric, cut:**

(2)  3⅞" (9.84cm) x WOF strips. From the strips, cut:
     (16) 3⅞" (9.84cm) squares

**From the blue fabric, cut:**

(2)  3⅞" x WOF strips. From the strips, cut:
     (16) 3⅞" (9.84cm) squares

**From the light purple, cut:**

(1)  4¾" (12.07cm) x WOF strip. From the strip, cut:
     (8) 4¾" (12.07cm) squares
(1)  7¼" (18.42cm) x WOF strip. From the strip, cut:
     (2) 7¼" (18.42cm) squares. Cut the squares in half diagonally twice to make (8) small setting triangles. Trim the remaining strip down to 4¾" (12.07cm) wide and cut:
     (5) 4¾" (12.07cm) squares.

**From the dark purple fabric, cut:**

(1)  4¾" (12.07cm) x WOF strip. From the strip, cut:
     (8) 4¾" (12.07cm) squares
(1)  7¼" (18.42cm) x WOF strip. From the strip, cut:
     (1) 7¼" (18.42cm) square. Cut the square in half diagonally twice to make (4) small setting triangles. Trim the remaining strip down to 4¾" (12.07cm) wide and cut:
     (2) 4¾" (12.07cm) squares.

**From the white fabric, cut:**

(4)  3⅞" (9.84cm) x WOF strips. From the strips, cut:
     (32) 3⅞" (9.84cm) squares
(8)  3⅞" (9.84cm) squares. Cut the squares on the diagonal to make (16) small corner triangles.
(3)  4¾" (12.07cm) x WOF strips. From the strips, cut:
     (24) 4¾" (12.07cm) squares
(1)  9⅞" (25.08cm) x WOF strip. From one of the strips, cut:
     (2) 9⅞" (25.08cm) squares. Cut the squares in half diagonally to make (4) large corner triangles.

Trim the remaining strip to 7¼" (18.42cm) wide, and cut:

(3) 7¼"(18.42cm) squares. Cut the squares in half diagonally twice to make (12) small setting triangles.

(1)  7¼" x WOF strip. From the strip, cut:

(2) 7¼" (18.42cm) squares. Cut the squares in half diagonally twice to make (8) small setting triangles.

(1)  13¼" (34.92cm) x WOF strip. From the strip, cut:

(2) 13¼" (34.92cm) squares. Cut in half diagonally twice to make (8) large setting triangles.

(3)  15½" (39.37cm) x WOF strips. From two of the strips, cut:

(2) 15½" x 39½" (39.37 x 100.33cm) rectangles From (1) strip, cut:

(1) 15½" (39.37cm) square.

Trim the remaining strip down to 13¼" (33.66cm) wide and cut:

(2) 13¼" (34.92cm) squares. Cut the squares in half diagonally twice to make (8) large setting triangles.

(1)  39½" (100.33cm) x WOF strip. From the strip, cut:

(1)  39½" (100.33cm) square

(8)  2½" (6.35cm) x WOF strips for binding

## MAKING THE HALF-SQUARE TRIANGLES (HST)

1.  Draw a diagonal line on the wrong side of (32) 3⅞" (9.84cm) white squares. Place a marked square, right sides together, on (1) 3⅞" (9.84cm) green square. Sew ¼" (0.64cm) away on both sides of the drawn line. Cut on the drawn line. Press seams toward the green triangle to make (2) 3½" (8.89cm) white/green HST units.

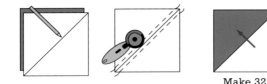

Make 32

2.  Place a marked square, right sides together, on (1) 3⅞" (9.84cm) blue square. Sew ¼" (0.64cm) away on both sides of the drawn line. Cut on the drawn line. Press seams toward the blue triangle to make (2) 3½" (8.89cm) white/blue HST units. Make (32.)

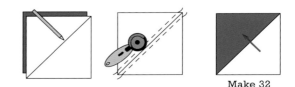

Make 32

## MAKING THREE-PATCH RECTANGLES

Sew (1) 4¾" (12.07cm) dark purple square between (2) 4¾" (12.07cm) white squares as shown. Press the seams toward the dark purple square to make a 4¾" x 13¼" (12.07 x 33.66cm) three-patch rectangle. Make (6) rectangles.

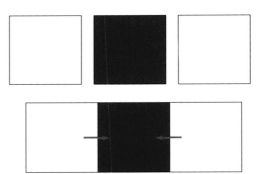

Make 6

## MAKING SMALL PIECED TRIANGLES

1.  Sew (1) white, small setting triangle to the top of (1) 4¾" (12.07cm) light purple square, as shown. Press the seam toward the white triangle.

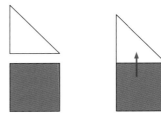

**FEARLESS TAKEAWAYS**

- Rather than centering a block and surrounding it by repeating borders, place the block in a corner of the design and add more background/open space in the opposite corner. This is an effortless way to incorporate negative space in a quilt that instantly creates a fresh look.

**CONFIDENCE BOOSTER**

- Don't bypass complex blocks with many pieces like the Sawtooth Squares block when considering options. When you substantially enlarge a complex block and only need to make a few, then the process is much less intimidating.

2. Sew a second white small setting triangle to the right of the square. Press the seam toward the white triangle to make a small pieced triangle. Make (4) triangles.

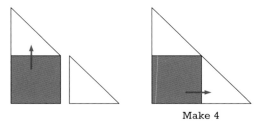

**Make 4**

LARGE PIECED TRIANGLES

1. Lay out (1) 4¾" (12.07cm) light purple square, (2) 4¾" (12.07cm) white squares, (2) light purple small setting triangles, and (1) dark purple small setting triangle in three rows, as shown.

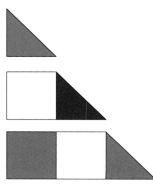

2. Sew the units in rows 2 and 3 together, pressing the seams in opposite directions. Join the rows, pressing the seams up.

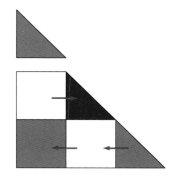

3. Sew the light purple triangle to the top of the unit. Press the seam up to make a large pieced triangle. Make (4) triangles.

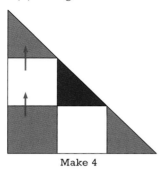

Make 4

## ASSEMBLING THE BLOCKS

1. For the center square, lay out
   (5) 4¾" (12.07cm) light purple squares,
   (4) 4¾" (12.07cm) dark purple squares,
   (4) 4¾" (12.07cm) white squares and
   (8) white small setting triangles in five diagonal rows, as shown.

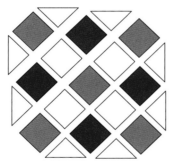

2. Sew the units together in each row. Press the seams in rows 1, 3 and 5 to the right. Press the seams in rows 2 and 4 to the left.

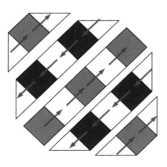

3. Join the rows and press the seams open. Sew a white small corner triangle to each of the corners. Press the seams toward the corner triangles to make the center square. Make (1) center block.

Make 1

## BLOCKS 1A & 1B

*(Keep blocks labeled "1A and 1B" as you sew pieces together.)*

1. Sew a white large setting triangle to the right of a small pieced triangle, as shown. Press the seam toward the setting triangle. (1) 15" x 18" (38.1 x 45.72cm) finished block for each type

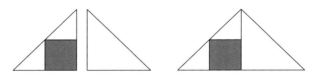

2. Sew a small setting triangle to the left of a three-patch rectangle. Press the seam toward the rectangle.

3. Sew the rectangle unit to the long side of the small pieced triangle unit from step 1. Press the seam open.

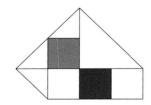

4. Sew a large white corner triangle to the bottom of the unit from step 3. Press the seam toward the triangle.

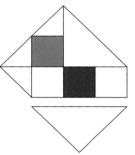

5. Sew a small white corner triangle to the end of the unit from step 4. Press the seam toward the small corner triangle.

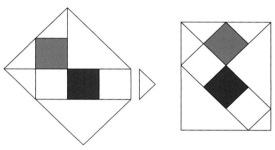

6. Sew (3) white/green HST units, alternating with (2) white/blue HST units, noting the orientation of the units. Press the seams in one direction to make a HST right side border.

7. Sew to the right side of the block. Press seams toward the HST border.

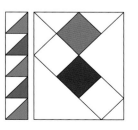

8. Repeat step 6 to make a left side border, paying attention to the orientation of HSTs. Sew the left side border to the left side of the unit from step 6 to make a 15½" x 18½" (39.37 x 46.99cm) Block 1A.

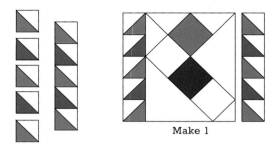

**Make 1**

9. Repeat steps 1–8, noting the new orientation of each of the units and the new right and left side border layouts, to make a 15½" x 18½" (39.37 x 46.99cm) Block 1B.

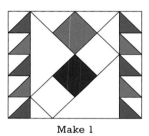

**Make 1**

## BLOCKS 2A & 2B

*(Keep blocks labeled "2A and 2B" as you sew pieces together.)*

1. Sew a large white setting triangle to the right of a large pieced triangle, aligning the bottom edges, as shown. Press the seam toward the setting triangle. (1)18" (45.72cm) finished block for each type

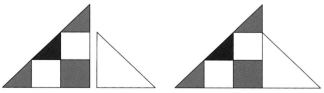

2. Sew a small white setting triangle to the left of a three-patch rectangle, as shown. Press the seam toward the rectangle.

3. Sew the rectangle unit to the right long side of the large pieced triangle unit from step 1, as shown. Press the seam open.

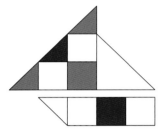

4. Sew a large white corner triangle to the bottom of the step 3 unit. Press the seam toward the triangle.

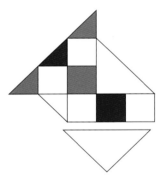

5. Sew a small white corner triangle to the end of the three-patch rectangle from the step 4 unit. Press the seam toward the small corner triangle.

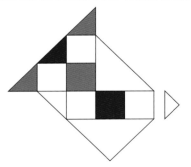

6. Sew (3) white/green HST units, alternating with (2) white/blue HST units, paying attention to the orientation of the units. Sew (1) white small

triangle to the top of the strip. Press the seams in one direction to make a HST right side border. Repeat to make a left side border, paying attention to the orientation of the units.

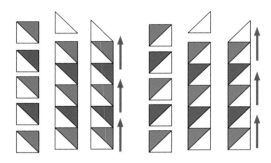

7. Following the illustration below, sew the right and left side borders to the block, starting at the bottom and sewing to ¼" (0.64cm) away from the inside corner of the top white/green HST. Leave the needle down and pivot the block. Continue sewing to the top corner of the block. Press the seams toward the side borders to make an 18½" (46.99cm) Block 2A. Make (1) block.

Make 1

8. Repeat the steps 1–6 to make Block 2B, paying attention to the new orientation of each of the units and the new right and left side border layouts to make an 18½" (46.99cm) Block 2B. Make (1) block.

Make 1

## BLOCKS 3A & 3B

*(Keep blocks labeled "3A" and "3B" as you sew pieces together.)*

1. Sew a large white setting triangle to the right of a large pieced triangle, aligning the bottom edges, as shown. Press the seam toward the setting triangle. (1) 8" x 21" (20.32 x 53.34cm) finished block for each type

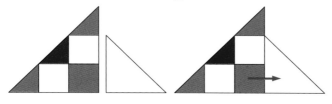

2. Sew a small setting triangle to the left and right end of a three-patch rectangle, as shown. Press the seams toward the rectangle. Sew the rectangle unit to the right long side of the large pieced triangle unit, as shown. Press the seam open.

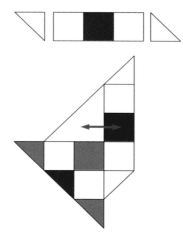

3. Sew a large white setting triangle to the right of a small pieced triangle, as shown. Press the seam toward the setting triangle.

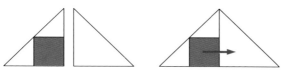

4. Sew the small pieced triangle unit to the bottom of the block unit from step 2. Press the seam toward the three-patch rectangle.

5. Sew (3) white/green HST units, alternating with (3) white/blue HST units, noting the orientation of the units. Sew (1) white small triangle to the top of the strip. Press the seams in one direction to make a HST right side border. Repeat to make a left side border, paying attention to the orientation of the units.

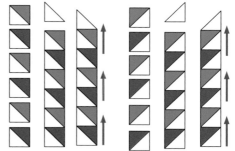

6. Following the illustration below, sew the right and left side borders to the block, starting at the bottom and sewing up to ¼" (0.64cm) away from the inside corner of the top white/blue HST. Leave the needle down and pivot the block. Continue sewing to the top corner of the block. Press the seams toward the side borders to make an 8½" x 21½" (46.99 x 54.61cm) Block 3A. Make (1) block.

7. Repeat the steps 1–6 to make Block 3B, paying attention to the new orientation of each of the units and the new right and left side border layouts, to make an 18½" x 21½" (46.99 x 54.61cm) Block 3B. Make (1) block.

Make 1

Make 1

## ASSEMBLING THE QUILT

1. Sew Block 1A between the 15½" (39.37cm) white square and (1) 15½" x 39½" (39.37 x 100.33cm) white rectangle as shown. Press the seams toward the white square and rectangle to make row 1.

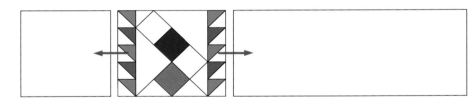

2. Lay out the Center Square, Block 1B, Block 3B and Block 2B, paying attention to the orientation of each block. Sew the blocks together. Press the seams open to make row 2.

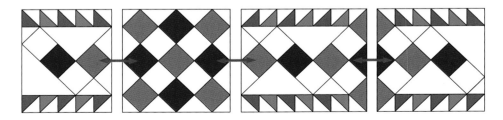

3. Sew Block 3A to the top of Block 2A as shown. Press the seam open. Sew the 3A/2A unit between (1) 15½" x 39½" (39.37 x 100.33cm) rectangle and the 39½" (100.33cm) white square. Press the seams toward the white rectangle and square to make row 3.

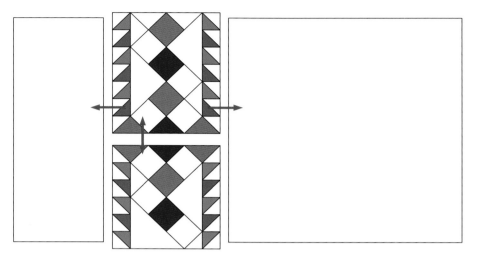

4. Sew row 2 between rows 1 and 3, matching the seams around the center square. Press the seams open to make a 72½" (182.88cm) quilt top.

## FINISHING THE QUILT

1. Layer the backing, batting and quilt top. Quilt as desired.

2. Trim the selvedge from each of the (8) binding strips. Sew together using diagonal seams to make one long strip. Press the seams open. Fold the binding in half, wrong sides together, and press along the entire length of the strip. Attach the binding using your preferred method.

**LEFT OF CENTER**
Finished size: 72" (182.88cm) square

# PARTICIPLE

In high school grammar, we were taught that dangling participles were bad, but in this case, the dangling rectangle became the central design element, thus. . . Participle.

I often like to try out various arrangements of traditional blocks when working with computer design software.

## MODERN

As I studied the quilt, I realized the blue rectangles just seemed to be dangling without any purpose which led to experimenting with over-exaggerating that element of the block.

## TRADITIONAL

The High Flying Squares block has a sense of movement, but I didn't like how the block appeared when simply set side by side.

## LEAP OF FAITH

- When a design element seems out of place, try either removing it completely or making it more prominent. This can often lead to a totally unique quilt that you didn't expect.

## COLOR LESSON

- This quilt incorporates an analogous color scheme, focusing on colors that are near each on a traditional color wheel. To make the design pop, consider using the lightest of your selected colors as backgrounds rather than white, beige, or another traditional background color.

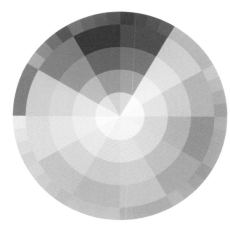

## MATERIALS
- ¼ yard (22.86cm) green
- 1 yard (91.44cm) blue
- 4¾ yards (365.76cm) yellow for quilt and binding
- 5 yards (457.2cm) for backing

WOF = width of fabric

## CUTTING
*Keep your cuts organized by size and color to make the block and quilt assembly easier.*

**From the green, cut:**
(3)  2½" (6.34cm) x WOF strips

**From the blue, cut:**
(8)  2½" (6.34cm) x WOF strips
(2)  4½" (11.43cm) x WOF strips

**From the yellow, cut:**
(13) 2½" (6.34cm) x WOF strips. From (3) strips, cut:
    (21) 2½" x 6½" (6.34 x 16.5cm) strips for blocks.
Reserve the extra strips for strip sets
(4)  4½" (11.43cm) x WOF strips. From (1) strip, cut:
    (5) 4½" (11.43 cm) squares
From one strip, cut:
    (1) 4½" x 39½" (36.83 x 100.33cm) rectangle for a bottom panel of quilt.
Piece the last 2 strips together end to end, and cut:
    (1) 4½" x 64" (11.43 x 162.56cm) strip for the top of the quilt
(10) 6½" (16.5cm) x WOF strips. From (1) strip, cut:
    (1) 6½" (16.5cm) square for Block C
    (3) 6½" x 10½" (16.5 x 26.67cm) rectangles for (3) Block A.
Sew (2) strips together, end to end, and cut:
    (1) 6½" x 49½" (16.5 x 124.46cm) strip for bottom panel of quilt.
Reserve the extra strips for strip sets and quilt segment.
(4)  10½" (26.67cm) x WOF strips. Mark the following cuts for the top section of quilt.
From (1) strip, cut:
    (1) 10½" x 4½" (26.67 x 11.43cm) rectangle
    (2) 10½" x 6½" (26.67 x 16.5cm) rectangles
    (1) 10½" x 18½" (26.67 x 46.99cm) rectangle
From (1) strip, cut:
    (1) 10½" x 12½" (26.67 x 31.75cm) rectangle
    (1) 10½" x 24½" (26.67 x 62.23cm) rectangle
Mark the following cuts for the bottom quilt section.
From (1) strip, cut:
    (1) 10½" x 31" (26.67 x 78.74cm) rectangle
    (1) 10½" x 4½" (26.67 x 11.43cm) rectangle

From (1) strip, cut:
- (1) 10½" x 22" (26.67 x 55.88cm) rectangle
- (1) 10½" x 13½" (26.67 x 34.29cm) rectangle
- (1) 10½" x 4½" (26.67 x 11.43cm) rectangle

**From the binding, cut:**
(8) 2½" (6.34 cm) x WOF strips

## MAKING THE BLOCK PANELS AND SEGMENTS

*Note: Keep segments labeled by size/color.*

Y/B/Y SEGMENTS

1. Sew (1) 2½" (6.34cm) x WOF blue strip between (1) 2½" (6.34cm) x WOF yellow strip and (1) 6½" (16.51cm) x WOF yellow strip to make a three-strip Y/B/Y panel. Press the seams in one direction. Make (5) 10½" (26.67cm) x WOF Y/B/Y panels.

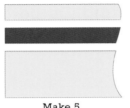

**Make 5**

2. Crosscut: (2) panels into (2) 29½" (74.93cm) lengths; (1) panel into (1) 2½" (6.34cm), (1) 4½" (11.43cm), (1) 6½" (16.51cm), and (1) 20" (50.8cm) length; (1) panel into (1) 25½" (64.77cm) length; (1) panel into (1) 8½"(21.59cm), and (1) 15" (38.1cm) length.

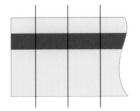

Y/B SEGMENTS

1. Sew (1) 2½" (6.34cm) x WOF blue strip to (1) 2½" (6.34cm) x WOF yellow strip to make a Y/B panel. Press the seams in one direction. Make (3) Y/B panels.

**Make 3**

2. Crosscut the (3) panels into (21) 4½" (6.34cm) segments.

G/B SEGMENTS

1. Sew (1) 2½" (6.34cm) x WOF green strip to (1) 4½" (6.34cm) x WOF blue strip to make a G/B panel. Press the seams in one direction. Make (2) G/B panels.

**Make 2**

2. Crosscut the panels into (21) 2½" x 6½" (6.34cm x 16.51cm) segments.

Y/G SEGMENTS

1. Cut (1) 2½" (6.34cm) x WOF green strip in half to make (2) 2½" x 21" (6.34 x 53.34cm) strips.
2. Cut (2) 2½" (6.34cm) x WOF yellow strips in half to make (4) 2½" x 21" (6.34 x 53.34cm) strips.

3. Sew (3) 2½" x 21" (6.34 x 53.34cm) yellow strips, alternating with (2) 2½" x 21" (6.34 x 53.34cm) green strips to make a five-strip Y/G panel. Make 2 Y/G panels.

4. Crosscut the (2) panels into (8) 2½" x 10½" (6.34 x 26.67cm) segments.

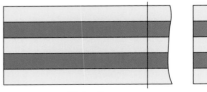

**Make 2**

## FEARLESS TAKEAWAYS

- While I seldom choose solid fabrics for my quilts, in this case, the design elements needed to remain crisp and clear. Print fabrics often muddy the edges of block design. While this is great for concealing less-than-perfect piecing, if you have a very strong design and want maximum visual impact, audition solid fabrics.

## CONFIDENCE BOOSTER

- When a traditional block, set side by side, isn't interesting, try replacing every other block with a plain background block. Having less visual distraction can identify areas that you can highlight to create a secondary design.

## MAKING THE BLOCKS

BLOCK A: (3) 10" (25.4CM) FINISHED BLOCKS

1. Sew (1) 2½" x 6½" (6.35 x 16.51cm) yellow rectangle to the left of (1) G/B segment. Press the seam toward the yellow rectangle.

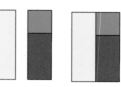

2. Sew (1) Y/B section to the top of the unit. Press the seam toward the Y/B section.

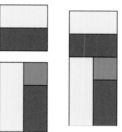

3. Sew (1) 6½" x 10½" (16.51 x 26.67cm) yellow rectangle to the right of the unit. Press the seam toward the yellow rectangle to make a 10½" (26.67cm) Block A. Make (3) blocks.

Make 3

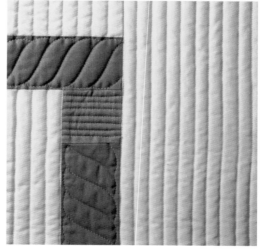

BLOCK B: (8) 10" (25.4cm) FINISHED BLOCKS

1. Sew (1) 2½" x 6½" (6.35 x 16.51cm) yellow rectangle to the left of (1) G/B segment. Press the seam toward the yellow rectangle. Make (2) rectangles.

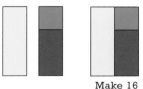

Make 16

2. Sew (1) Y/B section to the top of the unit. Press the seam toward the Y/B section. Make (2) sections.

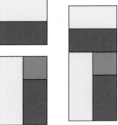

Make 16

3. Sew (1) Y/G segment between (2) units as shown. Press the seams open to make a 10½" (26.67cm) Block B. Make (8) blocks.

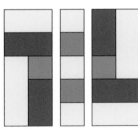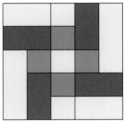

Make 8

BLOCK C: (1) 10" (25.4cm) FINISHED BLOCK

1. Sew (1) 2½" x 6½" (6.35 x 16.51cm) yellow rectangle to the left of (1) G/B segment. Press the seam toward the yellow rectangle. Make (2) rectangles.

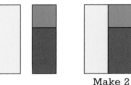

Make 2

2. Sew (1) Y/B section to the top of one unit. Press the seam toward the Y/B section. Sew (1) 6½" (16.51cm) yellow square to the right of the second unit from step 1. Press the seam toward the yellow square.

3. Sew the Y/B unit from step 2, to the top of the yellow square unit, as shown. Press the seam open to make a 10½" (26.67cm) Block C. Make (1) block.

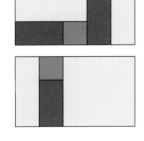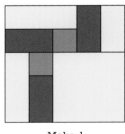

Make 1

47

## ASSEMBLING THE QUILT TOP SECTION

1. Referring to the Quilt Assembly Diagram 1, lay out (2) Block A, (4) of Block B, the (3) indicated Y/B/Y panels and the (5) indicated yellow rectangles in six vertical rows, noting the orientation of each block and panel.

2. Sew the units together in each vertical row. Press the seams in one direction. Join the rows from left to right. Sew the 4½" x 64" (11.43 x 162.56cm) yellow strip to the top of the quilt top section, trim if needed. Press the seams in one direction to make the top of the quilt.

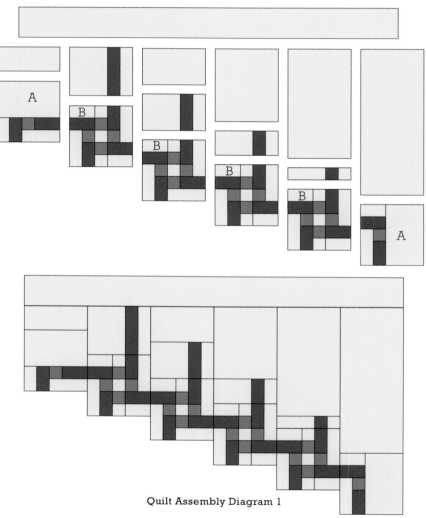

**Quilt Assembly Diagram 1**

## ASSEMBLING THE QUILT BOTTOM SECTION

1. Referring to the Quilt Assembly Diagram 2, lay out (1) Block A, (1) Block C, (4) Block B, (5) 4½" (11.43cm) yellow squares, the (5) indicated Y/B/Y panels and the (6) indicated yellow rectangles in seven vertical rows, noting the orientation of each block and panel.

2. Sew the units together in each vertical row. Press the seams in one direction. Join the rows from left to right. Press the seams in one direction to make the bottom of the quilt top.

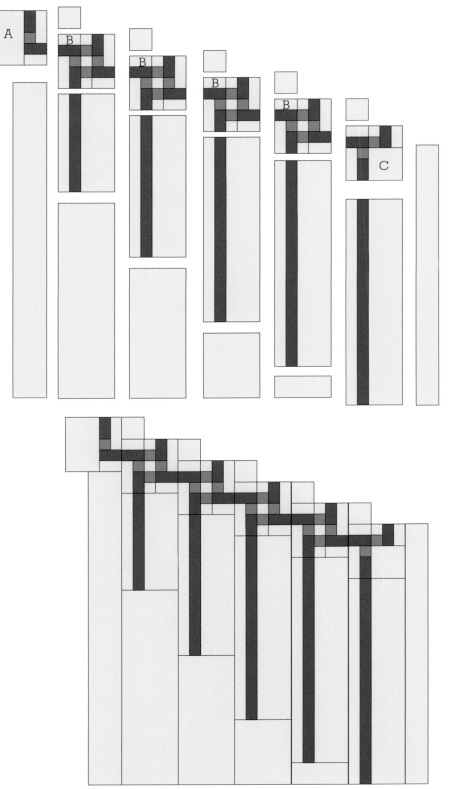

Quilt Assembly Diagram 2

## ATTACHING THE TOP AND BOTTOM OF THE QUILT

1. Sew the top of the quilt to the bottom of the quilt between the blocks by sewing from the left edge, matching the seams and stopping ¼" (0.634cm) from the corner of the first 4" (10.16cm) yellow square.

2. Leave the needle in the down position, pivot and sew down the 4" (10.16cm) yellow square to the bottom corner of the square. Leave the needle in the down position, pivot and sew across the next block.

3. Repeat the steps above, needle down and pivoting at each corner all the way across to the right side of the quilt. Press the seam open to complete the quilt top.

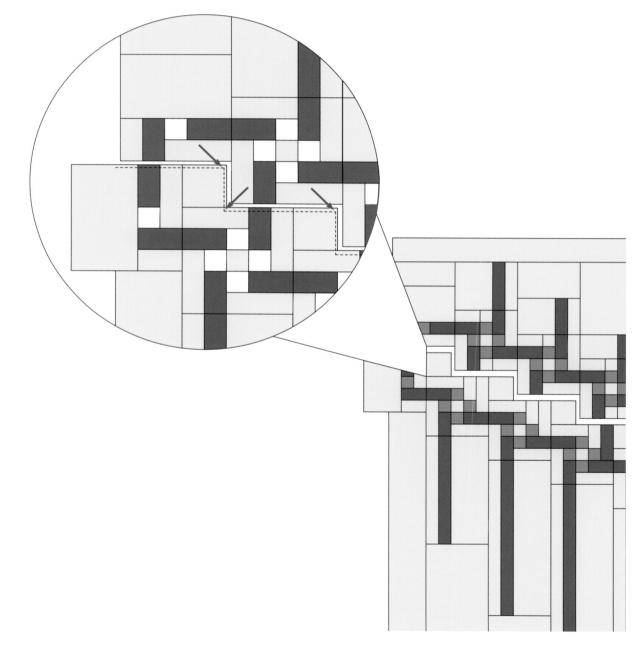

4. Trim the section of the left Block A, which extends outside of the right side of the quilt to align with the edge of the quilt.

**Finished Measurements**

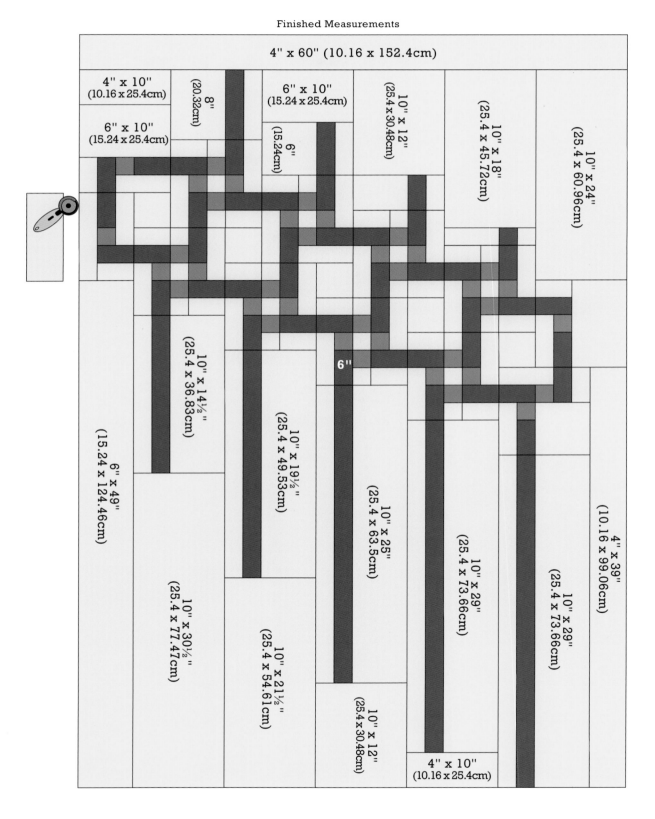

4" x 60" (10.16 x 152.4cm)

4" x 10" (10.16 x 25.4cm)

8" (20.32cm)

6" x 10" (15.24 x 25.4cm)

6" x 10" (15.24 x 25.4cm)

6" (15.24cm)

10" x 12" (25.4 x 30.48cm)

10" x 18" (25.4 x 45.72cm)

10" x 24" (25.4 x 60.96cm)

6"

10" x 14½" (25.4 x 36.83cm)

10" x 19½" (25.4 x 49.53cm)

6" x 49" (15.24 x 124.46cm)

10" x 30½" (25.4 x 77.47cm)

10" x 21½" (25.4 x 54.61cm)

10" x 25" (25.4 x 63.5cm)

10" x 29" (25.4 x 73.66cm)

10" x 29" (25.4 x 73.66cm)

4" x 39" (10.16 x 99.06cm)

10" x 12" (25.4 x 30.48cm)

4" x 10" (10.16 x 25.4cm)

## FINISHING THE QUILT

1. Cut the 5 yards (457.2cm) of backing fabric into (2) 90" (228.6cm) x WOF panels. Trim the selvedges from the yardage.

2. Using a ½" (1.27cm) seam allowance, sew the selvage edges of the 2 panels together to make the backing (seam will run vertically). Press the seam open.

3. Layer the quilt top, backing and batting. Quilt as desired.

4. Trim the selvedge from each of the (8) binding strips. Sew together using diagonal seams to make one long strip. Press the seams open. Fold the binding in half, wrong sides together, and press along the entire length of the strip. Attach the binding using your preferred method.

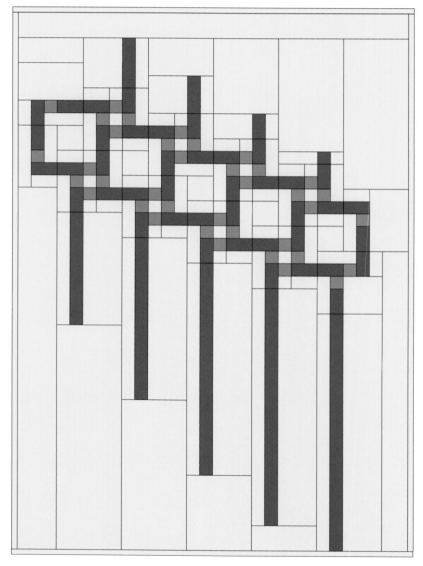

**PARTICIPLE**
Finished size: 60" x 77" (152.4 x 195.58cm)

# PARTY LIGHTS

By combining prints and batiks, and adding an angle to a traditional block, it creates an interesting design. The unique star shape of the block then reveals lots of design possibilities.

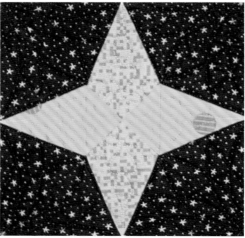

The classic pinwheel shape gains a modern edginess with the addition of another angle in one of the triangles and with a rainbow coloration and value progression along the diagonals.

## MODERN

Because this block has Y-seams, today's quilters often avoid it. But by adding an additional seam line, the block can be easily rotary cut and machine pieced.

To simplify block piecing, I added a seam line in the large trapezoid shape.

## TRADITIONAL

One of my favorite traditional blocks has always been the Periwinkle block, commonly seen in scrappy quilts from the 1930s.

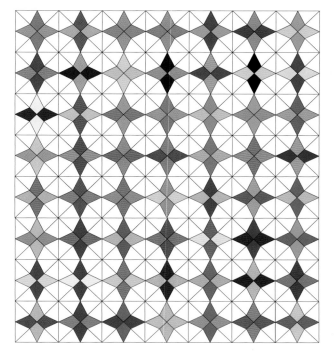

## LEAP OF FAITH

- While it may seem counterintuitive to add additional seams and, thus, more pieces to a block to simplify it, dividing a complex shape can make block piecing much easier. Don't be afraid to think outside the box and audition both fewer and more seams when evaluating how to make a block easier to achieve.

## COLOR LESSON

- By combining prints and batiks, I mixed styles and values using the color wheel approach. This block is best made with my acrylic template that just debuted.

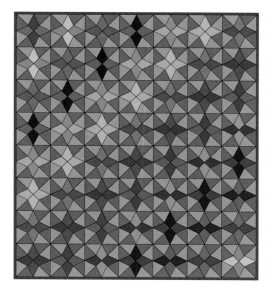

## MATERIALS
- ¼ yard (22.86cm) each of a rainbow of 24 different prints
- 5 yards (457.2cm) of background and binding print
- 5½ yards (502.92cm) for backing

WOF = width of fabric

## CUTTING

*NOTE: keep pieces organized by number to make it easier to piece the blocks. Use the A and B templates to cut block and background prints.*

**From the A prints, cut:**

Prints 1, 2, 3, 4, 5, 6, 23, 24:
　　(6) Template A diamonds from each print
Prints 7, 8, 21, 22:
　　(8) Template A diamonds from each print
Prints 9, 10, 19, 20:
　　(10) Template A diamonds from each print
Prints 11, 12, 17, 18:
　　(12) Template A diamonds from each print
Prints 13, 14, 15, 16:
　　(14) Template A diamonds from each print

**From the B Background print, cut:**

(28) 5" (12.7cm) x WOF strips. Leave fabric folded, and from each strip, cut:
　　(16) Template B triangles for a total of (448) background pieces.
(4)　4" (10.16cm) x WOF strips. From the strips, cut:
　　(37) 4" (10.16cm) Piece B squares for a total of (42) squares.
(9)　2½" (6.35cm) x WOF strips for binding

**From the dark blue, cut:**

(6)　4" (10.16cm) x WOF strips. From the strips, cut:
　　(57) 4" (10.16cm) Piece B squares.

*Label templates with letters through the completion of a block.*

| Fabric Pairs | Number of Blocks |
|:---:|:---:|
| 1–2 | 3 |
| 3–4 | 3 |
| 5–6 | 3 |
| 7–8 | 4 |
| 9–10 | 5 |
| 11–12 | 6 |
| 13–14 | 7 |
| 15–16 | 7 |
| 17–18 | 6 |
| 19–20 | 5 |
| 21–22 | 4 |
| 23–34 | 3 |

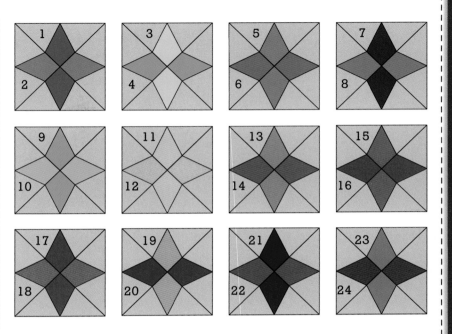

## MAKING THE BLOCKS

Refer to the chart above for how to pair fabric combinations. For example, use A fabric triangles 1 and 2, with B fabric triangles to make (3) blocks. (56) 9" (22.86cm) finished blocks

1. Sew the short side of a B Background triangle to the long side of an A fabric 1 diamond. Press seam open to reduce bulk.

2. Sew the short side a B Background triangle to the opposite long side of the A fabric 1 diamond from step 1, to make a quarter block unit. Press seam open to reduce bulk. Make (6) units.

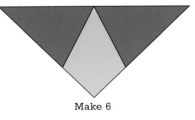

Make 6

3. Using 6 Fabric 2 diamonds, repeat steps 1–2 to make Fabric 2 quarter block units. Press seams open to reduce bulk. Make (6) units.

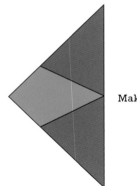

Make 6

- Adding seam lines can effectively simplify a block.

- Using a color progression approach effortlessly creates an updated look for a traditional block.

## CONFIDENCE BOOSTER

- An easy way to try a more modern color scheme is to simply use all colors. Pick a starting color and then use a color wheel as a guide to help you determine how to smoothly move from color to color.

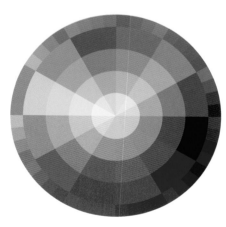

4. Sew a Fabric 1 quarter block to a Fabric 2 quarter block to make a half-block unit. Press seams open. Make (6) half-block units.

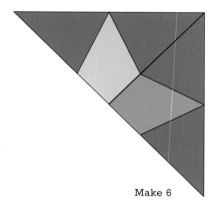

**Make 6**

5. Sew (2) half-block units together, carefully aligning seam intersections, to make a 9½" (24.13cm) unfinished block. Make (3) in this color combination.

6. Continue making blocks, referring to the chart, and following steps 1–5 to make (56) blocks.

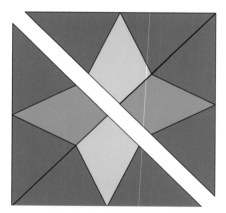

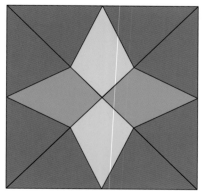

**Make 56**

# ASSEMBLING THE QUILT

Referring to the Quilt Assembly Diagram, lay out the (56) blocks in (8) rows of (7) blocks each, paying attention to color placement and orientation of the blocks. Sew the blocks together in rows, sew the rows together, pressing the seams open, to make a 63½" x 72½" (161.29 x 184.15cm) unfinished quilt top.

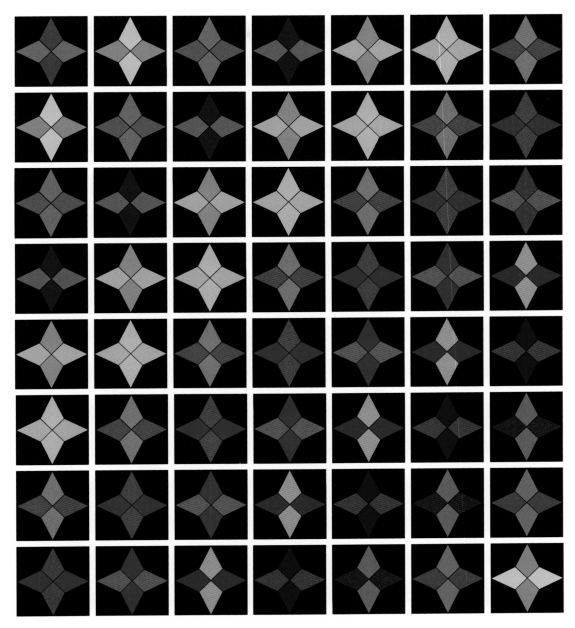

**Quilt Assembly Diagram**

## FINISHING THE QUILT

1. Cut the backing yardage into (2) 2¼"
   yards (205.74cm) x WOF pieces. Trim
   the selvedges.

2. Piece the (2) panels together along the
   long edge to make the backing.

3. Layer the quilt top, backing and batting.
   Quilt as desired.

4. Trim the selvedge from each of the
   binding strips. Sew together using
   diagonal seams to make one long
   strip. Press the seams open. Fold the
   binding in half, wrong sides together,
   and press along the entire length of
   the strip. Attach the binding using your
   preferred method.

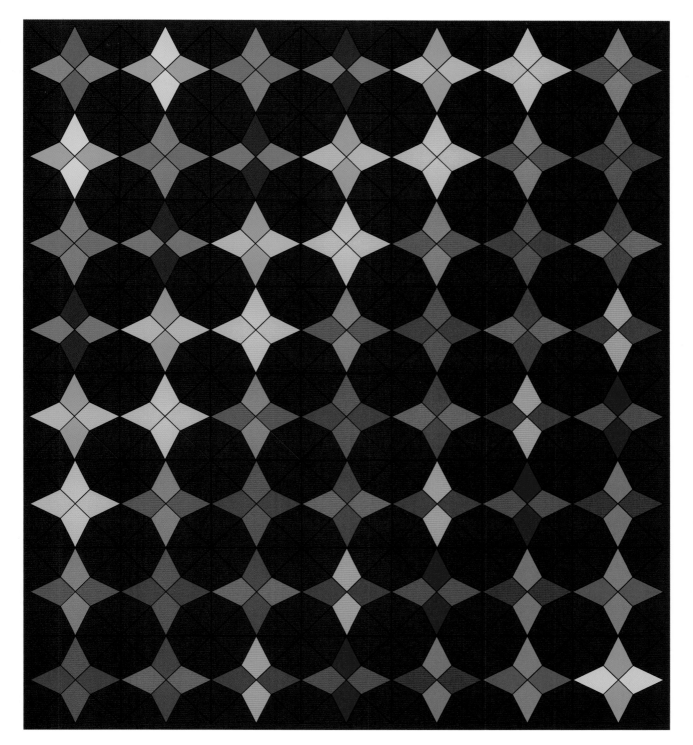

**PARTY LIGHTS**
Finished size: 64" x 73" (162.56 x 185.42cm)

# Party Lights Templates

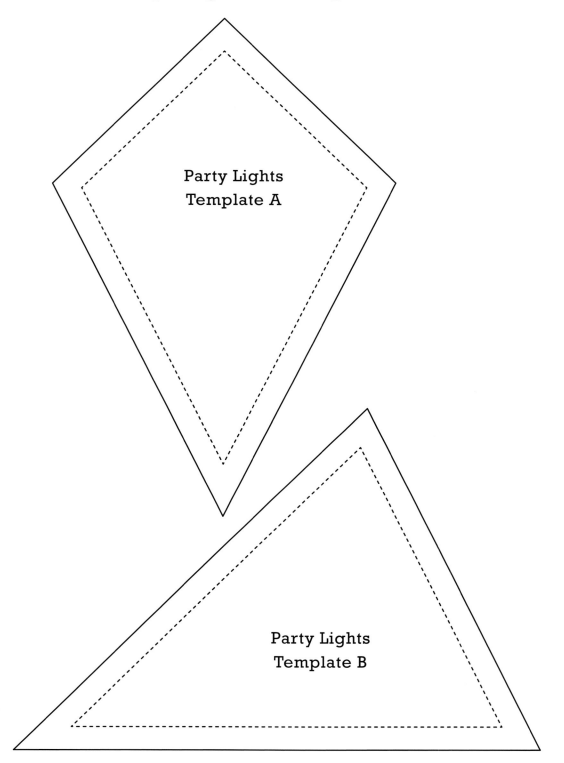

Party Lights
Template A

Party Lights
Template B

# PIECES OF ME

This quilt grew out of my interest in experimenting with "ghost" blocks—traditional patchwork blocks that are modernized by using background fabrics in places where the viewer would expect to see colored patches.

By piecing the shapes, rather than consolidating the patches into a large area of background, the overall outline of the block is preserved but it recedes into the background, becoming a ghost of the original. Incorporating a ghost element in parts of the background, however, immediately updates this block.

## MODERN

As an update, I incorporated a color progression approach within each block rather than across the entire quilt.

The quilt represents how taking time for one's self can add back color and joy to a life overwhelmed by daily stress. When we neglect ourselves, life can seem bleak and dark but as we slowly find ways to incorporate self-care, even if it's just by sewing for 15 minutes each day, we add back color until we restore balance.

## TRADITIONAL

The traditional block is unnamed according to vintage resources. It is repetitive and fairly uninteresting when set side by side.

## TRADITIONAL BLOCK

**From the purple, cut:**
(2)  6¼" (15.88cm) squares. Cut the squares twice, diagonally to make (8) Piece A triangles.
You'll use (7) in the quilt.

**From the binding fabric, cut:**
(8)  2-1/2" (6.35cm) x WOF strips

## FEARLESS TAKEAWAYS

- Replacing color patches with background fabric instantly updates traditional blocks.

## MATERIALS

*Refer to the color chips for help in choosing your fabrics. Keep your fabric organized by the letter/color designation.*

- 2 yards (182.66cm) Fabric A medium blue

- ¾ yard (68.58cm) Fabric B medium-dark blue

- ¾ yard (68.58cm) Fabric C dark blue

- ⅜ yard (34.29cm) EACH of colors:
    D light orange

    I mint

    J lime

    K orange

- ¼ yard (22.86cm) EACH of colors:
    E bright orange

    F red

    G bright pink

    H bright coral

    L lavender

    M teal

    N periwinkle

    O bright blue

    P turquoise

    Q pink

    R plum

    S purple

- 4 yards (365.76cm) backing fabric
- ⅔ yard (60.96cm) binding fabric

WOF = width of fabric

# CUTTING

The twenty blocks in this quilt are composed of eighteen colorations. Seventeen of the blocks are made once and the last block is made three times. I've included all the cutting in one chart, block construction techniques illustrating one block and then diagrams showing all the remaining blocks.

## From the medium blue print, cut:
(44) 6¼" (15.88cm) squares. Cut the squares twice diagonally to make (176) Piece A triangles. (You'll use 173 in the quilt.)

## From the medium-dark blue print, cut:
(3) 6¼" (15.88cm) squares.
     Cut the squares twice diagonally to make (12) Piece A triangles.
(42) 4" (10.16cm) Piece B squares

## From the dark blue, cut:
(57) 4" (10.16cm) Piece B squares

## From the light orange, cut:
(8) 6¼" (15.88cm) squares. Cut the squares twice diagonally to make (32) Piece A triangles.

## From the bright orange, cut:
(4) 6¼" (15.88cm) squares. Cut the squares twice diagonally to make (16) Piece A triangles.

## From the red, cut:
(4) 6¼" (15.88cm) squares. Cut the squares twice diagonally to make (16) Piece A triangles

## From the bright pink, cut:
(4) 6¼" (15.88cm) squares. Cut the squares twice diagonally to make (16) Piece A triangles

## From the bright coral, cut:
(4) 6¼" (15.88cm) squares. Cut the squares twice diagonally to make (16) Piece A triangles

## From the mint, cut:
(11) 6¼" (15.88cm) squares. Cut the squares twice diagonally to make (44) Piece A triangles. (You'll use (42) in the quilt.)

## From the lime, cut:
(11) 6¼" (15.88cm) squares. Cut the squares twice diagonally to make (44) Piece A triangles.

## From the orange, cut:
(8) 6¼" (15.88cm) squares. Cut the squares twice diagonally to make (32) Piece A triangles.

## From the lavender, cut:
(3) 6¼" (15.88cm) squares. Cut the squares twice diagonally to make (12) Piece A triangles. You'll use (10) in the quilt.
(9) 4" (10.16cm) Piece B squares

## From the teal, cut:
(3) 6¼" (15.88cm) squares. Cut the squares twice diagonally to make (12) Piece A triangles. (10) 4" (10.16cm) Piece B squares.

## From the periwinkle, cut:
(2) 6¼" (15.88cm) squares. Cut the squares twice diagonally to make (8) Piece A triangles.
(5) 4" (10.16cm) Piece B squares.

## From the bright blue, cut:
(2) 6¼" (15.88cm) squares. Cut the squares twice diagonally, to make (8) Piece A triangles.
(5) 4" (10.16cm) Piece B squares.

## From the turquoise, cut:
(2) 6¼" (15.88cm) squares. Cut the squares twice diagonally to make (8) Piece A triangles.
(7) 4" (10.16cm) Piece B squares.

## From the pink, cut:
(3) 6¼" (15.88cm) squares. Cut the squares twice diagonally to make (12) Piece A triangles.
(9) 4" (10.16cm) Piece B squares.

## From the plum, cut:
(2) 6¼" (15.88cm) squares. Cut the squares twice diagonally to make (8) Piece A triangles.
(5) 4" (10.16cm) Piece B squares.

## From the purple, cut:
(2) 6¼" (15.88cm) squares. Cut in half on both diagonals to yield (8) Piece A triangles.
 (7) 4" (10.16cm) Piece B squares.

## From the binding fabric, cut:
(8) 2½" (6.35cm) x WOF strips

## LEAP OF FAITH

- Ghost elements within a block add interest and a fresh feel. The simplest way to incorporate them is to pick two to three similar backgrounds that contrast significantly in tone or value from your print fabrics. Place these backgrounds in positions where you would expect to find prints so that element of the block recedes into the background, becoming a "ghost."

## CONFIDENCE BOOSTER

- Experiment with unexpected colorings within a block. Often we feel we have to balance color and print usage within a block in perfect symmetry—each rectangle has to be the same color; each triangle has to be another color. When we step away from those rules and try placing color and prints in new ways, unexpected and delightful things can happen.

MAKING THE BLOCKS

1. Follow the colorways of each block, shown below. Lay out the pieces needed. Each block contains (20) Piece A triangles and (8) Piece B squares. The blocks are assembled in diagonal rows.

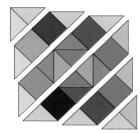

2. Make one each of blocks 1–15, 17 and 18. Block 16, 19 and 20 are made in the same colorway.

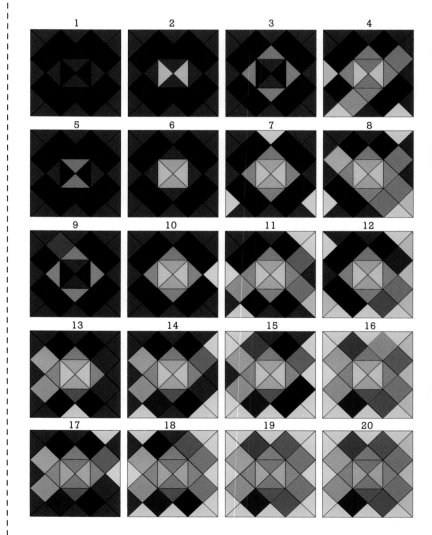

## ASSEMBLING THE QUILT

1. Referring to the Finished Size diagram, lay out (5) horizontal rows of (4) blocks each. Start with Block 1 in the upper left corner.

2. Sew the blocks together in rows and sew the rows together to complete the quilt top.

## FINISHING THE QUILT

1. Cut the backing yardage into 2 yards (182.88cm) x WOF pieces. Trim the selvedges.

2. Piece the (2) panels together along the long edge, using a ½" (1.27cm) seam, to make the backing.

3. Layer the quilt top, backing and batting. Quilt as desired.

4. Trim the selvedge from each of the (8) binding strips. Sew together using diagonal seams to make one long strip. Press the seams open. Fold the binding in half, wrong sides together, and press along the entire length of the strip. Attach the binding using your preferred method.

**PIECES OF ME**
Finished size: 62" x 77" (157.48 x 195.58cm)

# SHAZAM

The traditional Eight Point Star block has always been a favorite. But in my quest to create original, modern projects, I started wondering what if . . . .

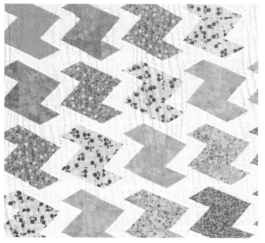

After experimenting with several options, I discovered this patch arrangement created a block that resembled a bolt of lightning.

## MODERN

What if that "Peaky and Spike" unit was rotated and moved out of the center position of the block?

What if the block was colored with just two fabrics—a background and a print.

What if a "spike" unit was colored with the same print as the "peaky" unit so an unusual shape appeared in the block?

What if the setting resembled the block shape with large areas of background and that same lightning shape.

## TRADITIONAL

Without the added background areas, a more traditional quilt would have rows of blocks, side by side like this.

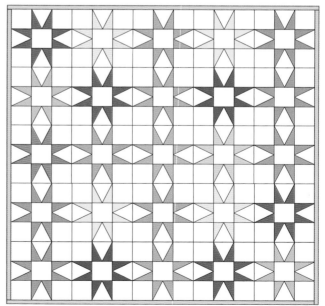

## LEAP OF FAITH

- When you are bored with traditional options, try mixing up color placement. Instead of placing fabrics where they "belong," put the same print next to itself when you wouldn't expect it to be there. Often, this will create a new shape your eye didn't see because of the standard grid lines.

- Use fewer or more fabrics than the traditional block calls for. Adding or subtracting fabrics can easily lead to new blocks by shifting what shapes emerge or recede.

## COLOR LESSON

- To soften and update rainbow or color progression palettes, choose varying value of a single color to move between the basic plan of red-purple-blue-green-yellow-orange.

- By adding softer or darker shades of the primary colors (move from pink to red to coral to orange), you can include more colors and make the transition between colors smoother.

- The Shazam quilt features my Prettiful Posies and Sew Sweet batik fabric lines.

## MATERIALS

*It's important to keep fabrics organized by size and letter to make it easier when cutting block pieces.*

- ⅛ yard (11.43cm) EACH of (5) assorted prints for blocks A, B, X, Y, Z
- ¼ yard (22.86cm) EACH of (15) assorted prints for blocks C through I and P through W
- ⅜ yard (31.75cm) EACH of (6) assorted prints for blocks J through O
- 7¼ yards (662.94cm) of a white print for background
- ¾ yard (68.58cm) of a light blue for binding
- 5½ yards (502.92cm) for backing

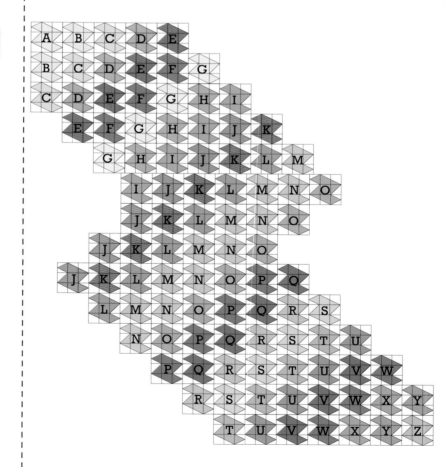

## PREPARATION:

Trace (1) each of Templates A–E, reversed to the template plastic to make a template pattern for cutting out block pieces. Cut out each template pattern on the drawn line.

Template A and Template C can be substituted by using a rotary cutter to cut 2½" (6.35cm) squares in place of Template A and 2⅞" (7.30cm) squares, cutting in half diagonally to make two triangles, in place of Template C for each block needed. Template D and Template E can be substituted by using a Tri-Recs™ ruler. Acrylic templates are also available.

## CUTTING

*Keep cuts organized by letter.*

### From Fabric A and Z, cut:
(1) Template A or (1) 2½" (6.35cm) square
(2) Template B
(2) Template C or (1) 2⅞" (7.30cm) square; cut once diagonally
(2) Template D
(1) Template E and (1) E reversed

### From Fabric B, X and Y, cut:
(2) Template A or (2) 2½" (6.35cm) squares
(4) Template B
(4) Template C or (2) 2⅞" (7.30cm) squares; cut once diagonally
(4) Template D
(2) Template E and (2) E reversed

### From Fabric C, D, F, H, V AND W, cut:
(3) Template A or (3) 2½" (6.35cm) squares
(6) Template B
(6) Template C or (3) 2⅞" (7.30cm) squares; cut once diagonally
(6) Template D
(3) Template E and (3) E reversed

### From Fabric E, G, I, P, Q, R, S, T and U cut:
(4) Template A or (4) 2½" (6.35cm) squares
(8) Template B
(8) Template C (4) 2⅞" (7.30cm) squares; cut once diagonally
(8) Template D
(4) Template E and (4) E reversed

### From Fabric J, K, L, M, N and O, cut:
(6) Template A or (6) 2½" (6.35cm) squares
(12) Template B
(12) Template C or (6) 2⅞" (7.30cm) squares; cut once diagonally
(12) Template D
(6) Template E and (6) E reversed

### From Fabric BG (background) fabric, cut :
(196) Template B
(196) Template C or (98) 2⅞" (7.30cm) squares; cut once diagonally
(294) Template E and (294) E reversed
(14) 6½" (16.51cm) x WOF strips

### From the binding fabric, cut:
(10) 2½" (6.35) x WOF strips

## MAKING THE BLOCKS
(98) 6" (15.24cm) FINISHED BLOCKS

1. Sew a BG Fabric, Template E to an A fabric, Template B, as shown. Press seam toward the BG fabric to make a 2½" (6.35cm) block unit. Make (2) block units.

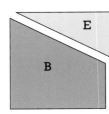

Make 2

2. Sew a BG Fabric, Template E to the left side of an A Fabric, Template D, as shown. Press the seam toward the BG Fabric triangle. Sew a BG Fabric, Template E-reversed, to the right side of template D, as shown. Press the seam toward the BG Fabric triangle to make a 2½" (6.35cm) block unit. Make (2) block units.

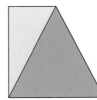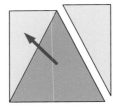

Make 2

## FEARLESS TAKEAWAYS

- Try different color options to see what shapes emerge. Start by working with only two colors—a light and a dark—and place those two colors in different positions to see what happens. If nothing excites you, add in a third or fourth color.

## CONFIDENCE BOOSTER

- Don't be afraid to move patchwork units around within a block, even swapping them out of their standard position. Rotating units can also create unexpected and interesting shapes. If you're not confident about computerized quilt design, cut shapes out of construction paper and play with them before cutting into your fabric.

3. Sew a BG Fabric, template C to an A Fabric, template C, as shown. Press the seam toward the A Fabric triangle to make a 2½" (6.35cm) block unit. Make (2) block units.

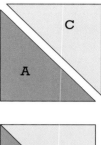

Make 2

4. Sew an A Fabric, template E, to a Fabric BG, template B, as shown. Press the seam toward the A Fabric triangle to make a 2½" (6.35cm) block unit. Make (2) block units.

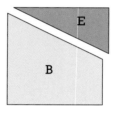

Make 2

5. Lay out the block units, as shown, and (1) A fabric square in three rows of three units each, as shown.

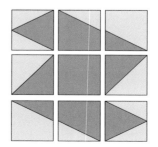

6. Sew the units together in each row. Press seams in rows 1 and 3 to the left. Press seams in row 2 to the right.

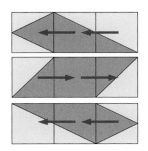

7. Sew the rows together and press the seams in one direction to make a 6½" (16.51cm) Fabric A quilt block. Make (1) block unit.

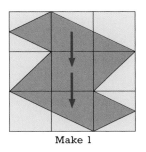

**Make 1**

8. Referring to the Block Chart, repeat steps 1–6, using the indicated fabric templates, A through E and background fabric templates, B, C, E and E-reversed, to make quilt blocks labeled with the fabric letter. Make an additional (97) blocks, using Fabrics B through Z.

| Fabrics | Blocks |
|---|---|
| B  with background | 2 |
| C  with background | 3 |
| D  with background | 3 |
| E  with background | 4 |
| F  with background | 3 |
| G  with background | 4 |
| H  with background | 3 |
| I  with background | 4 |
| J  with background | 6 |
| K  with background | 6 |
| L  with background | 6 |
| M  with background | 6 |
| N  with background | 6 |
| O  with background | 6 |
| P  with background | 4 |
| Q  with background | 4 |
| R  with background | 4 |
| S  with background | 4 |
| T  with background | 4 |
| U  with background | 4 |
| V  with background | 3 |
| W  with background | 3 |
| X  with background | 2 |
| Y  with background | 2 |
| Z  with background | 1 |

## ASSEMBLING THE QUILT

1. Sew the ends of (14) 6½" (16.51cm) x WOF, BG Fabric strips together to make a long strip. Crosscut the long strip into the following lengths:

(3) 6½" (16.51cm) squares
(4) 6½" x 12½" (16.51 x 31.75cm) strips
(5) 6½" x 18½" (16.51 x 46.99cm) strips
(4) 6½" x 24½" (16.51 x 62.23cm) strips
(3) 6½" x 30½" (16.51 x 77.47cm) strips
(2) 6½" x 36½" (16.51 x 92.71cm) strips
(1) 6½" x 42½" (16.51 x 107.95cm) strips
(1) 6½" x 48½" (16.51 x 123.19cm) strips

2. Refer to the Quilt Assembly Diagram; lay out the (98) blocks and the Fabric BG strips as shown in fourteen rows. Sew the blocks and strips together in each row. Press seams toward the BG Fabric strips.

3. Sew the rows together and press the seams in one direction to make a 78½" x 84½" (199.39 x 214.63cm) unfinished quilt top.

## FINISHING THE QUILT

1. Cut the backing yardage into (2) 2¾ yards (251.46cm) x WOF pieces. Trim the selvedges. Piece the 2 panels together along the long edge, using a ½" (1.27cm) seam, to make the backing. Press the seams open.

2. Layer the quilt top, backing and batting. Quilt as desired.

3. Trim the selvedge from each of the (10) binding strips. Sew together using diagonal seams to make one long strip. Press the seams open. Fold the binding in half, wrong sides together, and press along the entire length of the strip. Attach the binding using your preferred method.

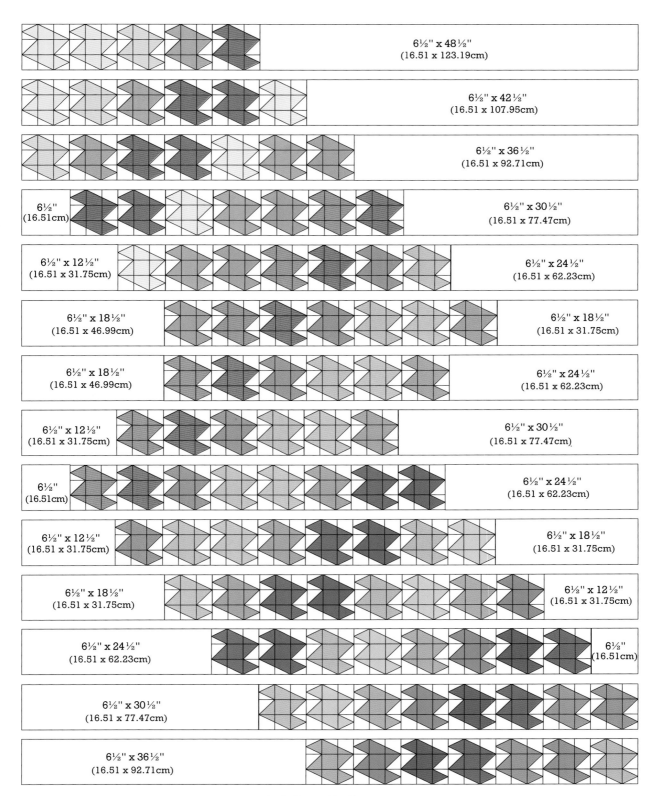

6½" x 48½"
(16.51 x 123.19cm)

6½" x 42½"
(16.51 x 107.95cm)

6½" x 36½"
(16.51 x 92.71cm)

6½"
(16.51cm)

6½" x 30½"
(16.51 x 77.47cm)

6½" x 12½"
(16.51 x 31.75cm)

6½" x 24½"
(16.51 x 62.23cm)

6½" x 18½"
(16.51 x 46.99cm)

6½" x 18½"
(16.51 x 31.75cm)

6½" x 18½"
(16.51 x 46.99cm)

6½" x 24½"
(16.51 x 62.23cm)

6½" x 12½"
(16.51 x 31.75cm)

6½" x 30½"
(16.51 x 77.47cm)

6½"
(16.51cm)

6½" x 24½"
(16.51 x 62.23cm)

6½" x 12½"
(16.51 x 31.75cm)

6½" x 18½"
(16.51 x 31.75cm)

6½" x 18½"
(16.51 x 31.75cm)

6½" x 12½"
(16.51 x 31.75cm)

6½" x 24½"
(16.51 x 62.23cm)

6½"
(16.51cm)

6½" x 30½"
(16.51 x 77.47cm)

6½" x 36½"
(16.51 x 92.71cm)

Quilt Assembly Diagram

# Shazam Templates

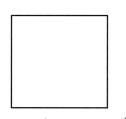

Be sure to compare the 1" (2.5cm) square on the template page to make sure you're printing at 100%. If the square is smaller or larger than 1" (2.5cm), adjust your printer percentage.

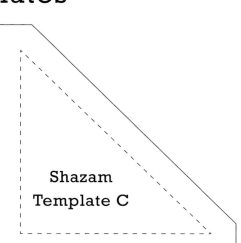

Shazam Template C

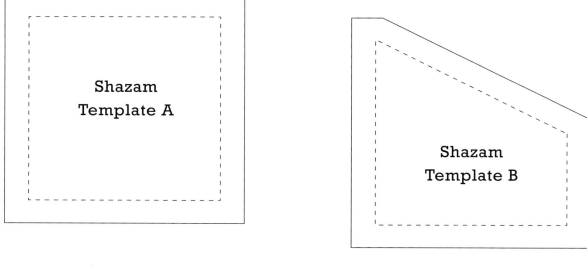

Shazam Template A

Shazam Template B

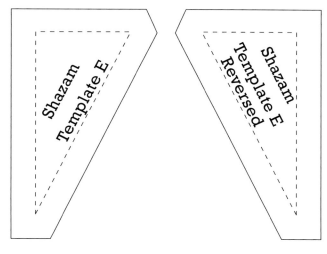

Shazam Template E

Shazam Template E Reversed

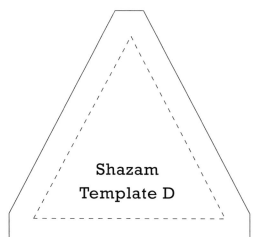

Shazam Template D

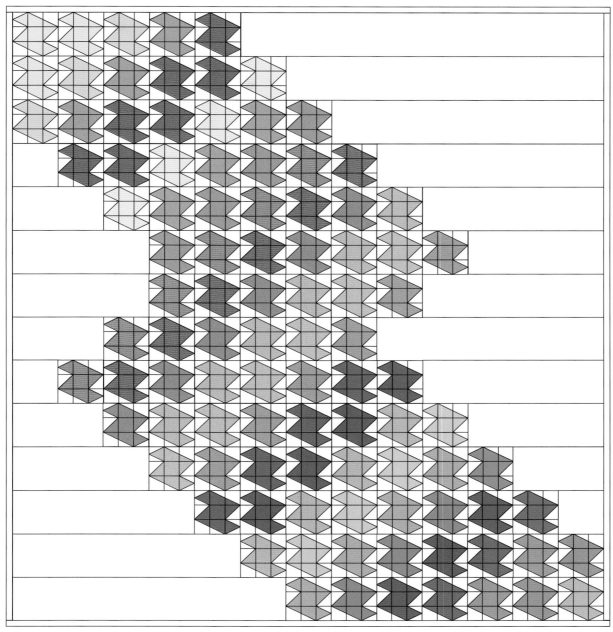

**SHAZAM**
Finished size: 78" x 84" (198.12 x 213.36cm)

# SPLIT PERSONALITY

Log Cabin blocks and their variations have endless possibilities since they can be rotated to create numerous secondary designs and patterns.

By subtracting some blocks from a traditional side-by-side set and adding negative space in the form of a patterned background print, this old favorite becomes the basis of an interesting, updated look.

## MODERN

By varying fabrics within blocks and removing some blocks entirely to add negative space into the quilt, a much more open, interesting design appears.

## TRADITIONAL

The traditional version of a repeated half log cabin block set side-by-side with every other block rotated 180 degrees looks like this: There is strong diagonal movement to the quilt but, overall, this quilt is only moderately interesting.

## LEAP OF FAITH

- The larger size of these blocks, along with the open areas of background, are the perfect opportunity to try two things in this quilt: 1) textured or heavier-weight fabrics, and 2) busy, large-scale prints. I combined various woven linens along with some traditional quilter's cottons in this quilt.

## COLOR LESSON

- A monochromatic color scheme adds immediate visual impact and puts the focus squarely on the design of the blocks. For this quilt, I selected shades of coffee, ranging from deep, dark espresso through the palest café au lait. The quilt will be equally effective when the full range of values of a single color are utilized—consider a quilt of blues ranging from deep navy to pale blue.

## MATERIALS

*Note: In terms of picking your own fabrics, look for a variation of value, considering that these prints are next to each other in the various blocks.*

- 1¼ yard (102.87cm) Fabric A large-scale print for block centers
- ½ yard (45.72cm) Fabric B medium print for blocks
- 2¼ yards (205.74cm) Fabric C dark print for blocks and binding
- 3¼ yards (284.48cm) Fabric D background fabric
- 1 yard (91.44cm) Fabric E large-scale print for block centers
- 6 yards (548.64cm) of backing

WOF = width of fabric

THE BLOCKS INCLUDE THREE DIFFERENT FABRIC COMBINATIONS

Block 1, make 6    Block 2, make 8    Block 3, make 10

## CUTTING

*Note: Keep pieces organized by color and size.*

**From the Fabric A large-scale print, cut:**
(4)  9½" (24.13cm) x WOF strips. From the strips, cut:
    (14) 9½" (24.13cm) squares

**From the Fabric B medium print, cut:**
(4)  3½" (8.89cm) x WOF strips. From 2 strips, cut:
    (6) 3½" x 12½" (8.89 x 31.75cm) rectangles
    From the remaining B medium print strips, cut:
    (6) 3½" x 9½" (8.89 x 24.13cm) rectangles

**From Fabric C dark print, cut:**
(16) 3½" (8.89cm) x WOF strips.
From 8 strips, cut:
    (24) 3½" x 12½" (8.89 x 31.75cm) rectangles
From 3 strips, cut:
    (6) 3½" x 15½" (8.89 x 26.67cm) rectangles
From 5 strips, cut:
    (18) 3 ½" x 9 ½" (8.89 x 24.13cm) rectangles
    (10) 2-1/2" (6.35cm) x WOF strips for the binding

**From the Fabric D background print, cut:**
(3)  15½" (26.67cm) x WOF strips. From (2) strips, cut:
    (2) 15½" x 30½ (26.67 x 77.47cm) rectangles
    (2) 15½" (26.67cm) squares
(15) 3½" (8.89cm) x WOF strips.
From (9) strips, cut:

(18) 3½" x 15½" (8.89 x 26.67cm) rectangles
From 6 strips, cut:
    (18) 3½" x 12½" (8.89 x 31.75cm) rectangles

**From Fabric E large sale print, cut:**
(3)  9½" (24.13cm) x WOF strips.
    From the strips, cut:
    (10) 9½" (24.13cm) squares

## MAKING THE BLOCKS

BLOCK 1: (6) 15" (38.1CM) FINISHED BLOCKS

1. With right sides together, sew a fabric B
   3½" x 9½" (8.89 x 24.13cm) rectangle to the
   side of a Fabric A square. Sew along the side
   and press the seam toward the rectangle.

2. Sew a fabric B, 3½" x 12½" (8.89 x 31.75cm)
   rectangle to the side of the unit from step 1, as
   shown. Press seams toward the rectangle.

3. Sew a fabric C, 3½" x 12½" (8.89 x 31.75cm)
   rectangle to the short side of the unit from step
   2. Press the seam toward the rectangle.

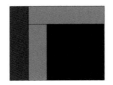

4. Sew a fabric C, 3½" x 15½" (8.89 x 26.67cm)
   rectangle to the pieced unit, paying attention
   to orientation. Repeat steps 1–4 to make (6)
   Block 1.

Make 6, Block 1

BLOCK 2: (8) 15" (38.1CM) FINISHED BLOCKS

1. With right sides together, sew a fabric C
   3½" x 9½" (8.89 x 24.13cm) rectangle to the side
   of a Fabric A square. Sew along the side and
   press the seam toward the rectangle.

2  Sew a fabric C, 3½" x 12½" (8.89 x 31.75cm)
   rectangle to the side of the unit from step 1, as
   shown. Press seams toward the rectangle.

3. Sew a fabric D, 3½" x 12½" (8.89 x 31.75cm)
   rectangle to the short side of the unit from step
   2. Press the seam toward the rectangle.

4. Sew a fabric D, 3½" x 15½" (8.89 x 26.67cm)
   rectangle to the pieced unit, paying attention
   to orientation. Repeat steps 1–4 to make (8)
   Block 2.

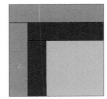

Make 8, Block 2

## FEARLESS TAKEAWAYS

- Adding more background/ negative space to a quilt design in lieu of pieced patches can quickly update a traditional design.

- Non-traditional fabrics such as linens or wovens can be successfully used in quilts, especially if you work with a larger overall scale to your block design and patchwork pieces.

## CONFIDENCE BOOSTER

- A traditional block like a half Log Cabin has a lot of design potential because it can be rotated to create different, intersecting effects. Start by rotating every other block 90 degrees, then 180 degrees and then 270 degrees to see what new patterns emerge. Fine-tune the design by removing some blocks altogether.

## ALTERNATIVE COLORWAY

BLOCK 3: (6) 15" (38.1CM) FINISHED BLOCKS

1. With right sides together, sew a fabric C, 3½" x 9½" (8.89 x 24.13cm) rectangle to the side of a Fabric E square. Sew along the side and press the seam toward the rectangle.

2  Sew a fabric C, 3½" x 12½" (8.89 x 31.75cm) rectangle to the side of the unit from step 1, as shown. Press seams toward the rectangle.

3. Sew a fabric D, 3½" x 12½" (8.89 x 31.75cm) rectangle to the short side of the unit from step 2. Press the seam toward the rectangle.

4. Sew a fabric D, 3½" x 15½" (8.89 x 26.67cm) rectangle to the pieced unit, paying attention to orientation. Repeat steps 1–4 to make (10) Block 3.

**Make 10, Block 3**

# MAKING THE QUILT TOP

1. Following the Quilt Assembly Diagram, lay out the background rectangles and blocks, as shown, paying attention to orientation of the blocks.

2. Sew together in rows and sew the rows together to finish the quilt top.

## FINISHING THE QUILT

1. Cut the backing yardage into (2) 3 yard (274.32cm) x WOF pieces. Trim the selvedges from the yardage.

2. Piece the (2) panels together along the long edge, using a ½" (1.27cm) seam, to make the backing.

3. Layer the quilt top, backing and batting. Quilt as desired.

4. Trim the selvedge from each of the (10) binding strips. Sew together using diagonal seams to make one long strip. Press the seams open. Fold the binding in half, wrong sides together, and press along the entire length of the strip. Attach the binding using your preferred method.

**SPLIT PERSONALITY**
Finished size: 77" x 92" (195.58 x 233.68cm)

# SWIRLY WHIRL

Pinwheel-style blocks have long been interesting to me. As I studied the Double Pinwheel block, I started wondering what would happen if the slant of the angle was changed to create a more interesting dynamic.

One of my favorite blocks is the Pinwheel block.

## MODERN

By having some variation in the angles, the design options are suddenly expanded and the quilt design seems more open.

To further highlight the design elements, I decided to incorporate a color wash effect with both the prints and the backgrounds. The result is an interesting design perfect for showcasing a huge variety of fabrics.

## TRADITIONAL

A traditional Double Pinwheel quilt has some movement but can appear very busy, making it hard to focus on any one pinwheel shape.

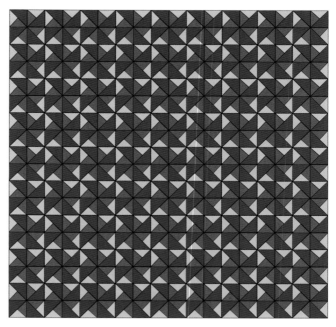

## LEAP OF FAITH

- Don't be afraid to try out a pattern that isn't perfect—it may just be the spark your quilt needs.

## COLOR LESSON

- Part of the appeal of Swirly Whirl is the extensive use of color. I pulled together collections from three different designers for this quilt. The lines ranged from very clear, cool colors to warmer, muddier hues. The overall effect works because there are so many fabrics used and the slightly "off" shades appear in smaller quantities.

## MATERIALS

*Refer to the Block Chart, page 93, for color ideas.*

**One Fat Quarter EACH**
**18" x 22"**
**(45.72 x 55.88cm)**

- Lt/Med Red #1
- Lt/Med Red #2
- Med/Dk Red #1
- Med/Dk Red #3
- Lt/Med Blue #3
- Med/Dk Blue #3
- Med/Dk Sage #1
- Med/Dk Sage #2
- Med/Dk Sage #3
- Med/Dk Gold
- Med/Dk Orange
- Lt/Med Turquoise
- Med/Dk Turquoise
- Lt Gray
- Med Gray #2

**⅞ yard (80.01cm) EACH**

- Lt/Med Pink #1
- Lt/Med Blue #1
- Lt/Med Blue #2
- Lt/Med Purple #1
- Lt/Med Purple #2

**½ yard (45.72cm) EACH**

- Med/Dk Green
- Med/Dk Pink #2
- Med/Dk Red #2
- Lt/Med Gold
- Lt/Med Sage #2
- Med/Dk Blue #1
- Med/Dk Pink #1
- Med/Dk Purple #1
- Med Gray #1
- Dk Gray #1
- Dk Gray #3
- Black #2

**⅝ yard (57.15cm) EACH**

- Lt/Med Orange
- Med/Dk Blue #2
- Med/Dk Purple #2
- Lt/Med Sage #1
- Lt/Med Green
- Lt/Med Pink #2
- Dk Gray #2
- Black #1

**2⅝ yard (189.23cm)**

- White

- 1 yard (91.44cm) of a black print for binding
- 9-3/4 (891.54cm) yards for backing
WOF = width of fabric

# CUTTING

*Keeping the strips labeled with their color names/number will make it easier to cut block pieces.*

## FAT QUARTER CUTS

**Cut (1) 6½" x 21" (16.51 x 53.34cm) of EACH following colors:**
Lt/Med Red #1
Med/Dk Red #1
Lt/Med Turquoise
Med/Dk Turquoise
Lt Gray
Med Gray #2

**Cut (2) 6½" x 21" (16.51 x 53.34cm) of EACH following colors:**
Lt/Med Red #2
Med/Dk Red #3
Lt/Med Blue #3
Med/Dk Blue #3
Lt/Med Sage #3
Med/Dk Sage #1
Med/Dk Sage #2
Med/Dk Orange

## WIDTH OF FABRIC (WOF) CUTS

### ½ YARD (45.72CM) CUTS

**Cut (2) 6½" (16.51cm) x WOF strips of the following colors:**
Med/Dk Red #2
Lt/Med Gold
Med/Dk Gold
Lt/Med Sage #1
Med/Dk Green
Med/Dk Pink #2
Med/Dk Blue #1
Med/Dk Pink #1
Med/Dk Purple #1
Lt/Med Sage #2
Med Gray #1
Dk Gray #1
Black #2
Dk Gray #3

### ⅝ YARD (57.15CM) CUTS

**Cut (3) 6½" (16.51cm) x WOF strips of the following colors:**
Lt/Med Sage #1
Lt/Med Orange
Lt/Med Green
Lt/Med Pink #2
Med/Dk Blue #2
Med/Dk Purple #2
Dk Gray #2
Black #1

### ⅞ YARD (80.01CM) CUTS

**Cut (4) 6½" (16.51cm) x WOF strips of the following colors:**
Lt/Med Blue #1
Lt/Med Pink #1
Lt/Med Blue #2
Lt/Med Purple #2

**From lt/med Purple #1, cut :**
(5) 6½" (16.51cm) x WOF strips

**From the white fabric, cut :**
(14) 6½" (16.51cm) x WOF strips

**From the binding, cut:**
(12) 2½" (6.35cm) x WOF strips

## MAKING THE BLOCKS
(81) 12" (30.48CM) FINISHED BLOCKS

*NOTE: All the blocks in the quilt are made following the step by step below. Color pieces use A and C templates. White, Gray, or Black pieces use the B template. The blocks will always have (2) white B triangles and (2) black or gray B triangles.*

Use the block cutting chart on page 93 to cut pieces from fat quarters and WOF cut strips. Follow steps 1–6, paying attention to color and quarter-block orientation, to make (81) 12½" (31.75cm) blocks.

1. Sew (1) Template C triangle (color) to (1) Template B triangle (gray or black) as shown.

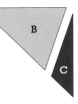

   Press the seam toward the Template B triangle.

2. Sew the C/B pieced triangle to a Template A triangle. Press the seam toward the Template A triangle to make a 6½" (16.51cm) square. Make (2) squares.

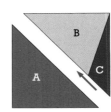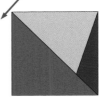

   Make 2

## FEARLESS TAKEAWAYS

- Varying both the color progression of prints and the value progression of background fabrics adds visual complexity to a simple pieced block.

## CONFIDENCE BOOSTER

- Because this block features triangle shapes you may not have sewn before, consider cutting out a test block and piecing before cutting everything. For maximum accuracy, I often mark dots where the angles of lines intersect and then pin those dots and use them as reference points when joining seams. Acrylic templates are available to aid with this method.

3. Sew a Template C triangle (color) to a Template B triangle (white) as shown. Press the seam toward the Template B triangle.

4. Sew the C/B pieced triangle to (1) Template A triangle (color). Press the seam toward the Template A triangle to make a 6½" (16.51 cm) square. Make (2) squares.

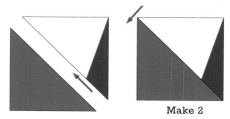

**Make 2**

5. Lay out (4) quarter-triangles in two rows, noting the color orientation and placement of each. Sew the quarter-blocks together in each row. Press the seams open to reduce bulk in the block center.

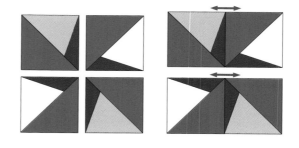

6. Join the rows. Press the seams open to make a 12½" (31.75 cm) block.

# BLOCK CHART

Template A, cut
(4) lt/med red #1

Template B, cut
(2) lt gray, (2) white

Template C, cut
(4) med/dk red #1

Template A, cut:
(28) lt/med blue #1

Template B, cut:
(7) dk gray #1,
(7) dk gray #2,
(14) white

Template C, cut:
(28) med/dk blue #1

Template A, cut:
(20) lt/med orange

Template B, cut:
(5) black #2
(5) dk gray #3
(10) white

Template C, cut:
(20) med/dk orange

Template A, cut:
(8) lt/med red #2

Template B, cut:
4) lt gray, (4) white

Template C, cut:
(8) med/dk red #2

Template A, cut:
(32) lt/med blue #2

Template B, cut:
(16) dk gray #2
(16) white

Template C, cut:
(32) med/dk blue #2

Template A, cut:
(16) med/dk gold

Template B, cut:
(8) dk gray #3
(8) white

Template C, cut:
(16) med/dk sage #2

Template A, cut:
(12) med/dk red #2

Template B, cut:
(3) lt gray,
(3) med gray #1
(6) white

Template C, cut:
(12) med/dk red #3

Template A, cut:
(36) lt/med purple #1

Template B, cut:
(9) dk gray #2,
(9) black #1,
(18) white

Template C, cut:
(36) med/dk purple #1

Template A, cut:
(12) lt/med sage

Template B, cut:
(3) dk gray #3
(3) med gray #2
(6) white

Template C, cut:
(12) med/dk sage #3

Template A, cut:
(16) lt/med gold

Template B, cut:
(8) med gray #1
(8) white

Template C, cut:
(16) med/dk gold

Template A, cut:
(40) lt/med purple #2

Template B, cut:
(20) black #1,
(20) white

Template C, cut:
(40) med/dk red #3

Template A, cut:
(8) lt/med blue #3

Template B, cut:
(4) med gray #2
(4) white

Template C, cut:
(8) med/dk blue #3

Template A, cut:
(20) lt/med sage #1

Template B, cut:
(5) med gray #1,
(5) dk gray #1,
(2) white

Template C, cut:
(20) med/dk sage

Template A, cut:
(28) Lt/Med Pink #1

Template B, cut:
(7) Black #1,
(7) Black #2
(14) White

Template C, cut:
(28) Med/Dk Pink #1

Template A, cut:
(4) lt/medturquoise

Template B, cut:
(1) med gray #2
(1) med gray #1
(2) white

Template C, cut:
(4) med/dk turquoise

Template A, cut:
(24) lt/med green

Template B, cut:
(12) dk gray #1,
(12) white

Template C, cut:
(24) med/dk green

Template A, cut:
(24) lt/med pink #2

Template B, cut:
(12) black #2
(12) white

Template C, cut:
(24) med/dk pink #2

# PROJECTS

## ASSEMBLING THE QUILT TOP

1. Referring to the Quilt Assembly Diagram, lay out the blocks in nine rows of nine blocks each, noting the orientation of each block. (*Note: where the blocks intersect, a gray (or black) or white star will be formed.*)

2. Sew the blocks together in rows. Press the seams open to reduce bulk at the seam intersections. Join the rows. Press the seams open to make a 108½" x 108½" (275.59 x 275.59cm) quilt top.

3. Sew the rows together to finish the quilt top. Press the seams open to make a 108½" (275.59cm) square quilt top.

## FINISHING THE QUILT

1. Cut the 9¾ yards (891.54cm) of backing fabric into (3) 3¼ yard (297.18cm) panels. Trim the selvedges from the yardage.

2. Sew the (3) panels together along the selvedge edge, using a ½" (1.27cm) seam, to make the backing approximately 117" (297.18cm) square. The backing seams should run vertically. Press the seams open.

3. Layer the quilt top, backing and batting. Quilt as desired.

4. Trim the selvedge from each of the (12) binding strips. Sew together using diagonal seams to make one long strip. Press the seams open. Fold the binding in half, wrong sides together, and press along the entire length of the strip. Attach the binding using your preferred method.

**Quilt Assembly Diagram**

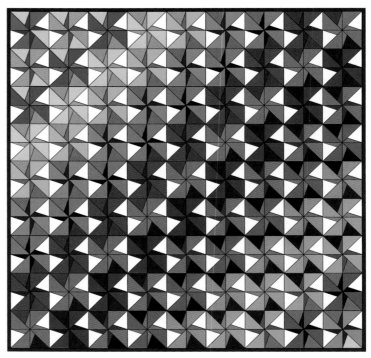

**SWIRLY WHIRL**
Finished size: 108" (274.32cm) square

# Swirly Whirl Templates

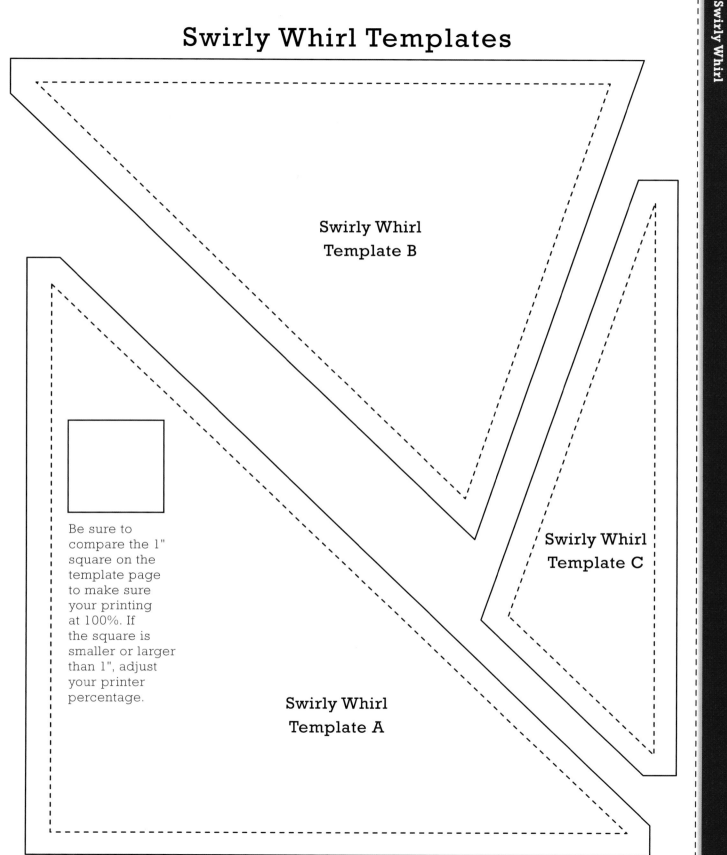

Swirly Whirl
Template B

Swirly Whirl
Template C

Swirly Whirl
Template A

Be sure to compare the 1" square on the template page to make sure your printing at 100%. If the square is smaller or larger than 1", adjust your printer percentage.

# GRIDDED GARDEN

When I first started playing with the traditional Gothic block,
I loved the diagonal movement and how different aspects of the
block stood out depending on how shapes were colored.

Enlarging the block size and simplifying piecing was the first step to updating this traditional block. I doubled the block from 16" to 32" (40.64 to 81.28cm).

## MODERN

I incorporated easier stitching techniques, including stitch and flip triangles, to eliminate some of the seams.

Finally, adding solids in place of some of the prints and varying the print used in the sashing gave this quilt design a fresh feel. This made the flower shapes within the blocks stand out. The result is the Gridded Garden quilt.

## TRADITIONAL

A very traditional rendering of this block looked like this in my early design phase. But when I calculated the pieces needed to make the quilt, I paused—each block had 108 pieces. At 25 blocks, that would be 2,700 pieces to cut and sew back together.

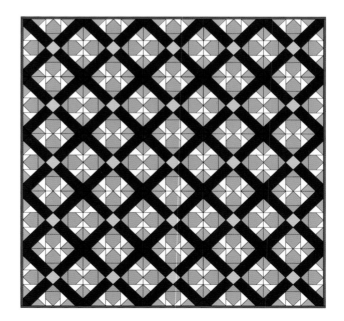

## LEAP OF FAITH

- As a long-time traditional quilter, it was a leap for me to pair solid fabrics with prints. But solids add an instant modern look to a quilt design, and provide a needed visual resting place when mixed with busy prints. Once you've settled on a palette and focal fabrics for your quilt, add in two to three solids in the supporting roles. Having more than one solid makes the design decision appear intentional rather than random, and contributes to a more cohesive look.

## ALTERNATIVE COLORWAY

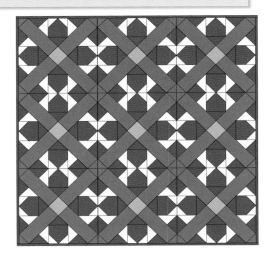

## CONFIDENCE BOOSTER

- **PRO TIP:** I pin a small square of paper to each set of cut pieces indicating what that piece is—"Piece A Squares," "Piece B triangles," etc.

## MATERIALS:

- 1¾ yards (160.02cm) large-scale floral print
- 1½ yards (137.16cm) medium-scale floral print
- ¼ yard (22.86cm) yellow print
- ¼ yard (22.86cm) multi-white print
- 1⅝ yards (148.59cm) dark teal solid
- 1⅜ yards (125.73cm) bright teal solid
- 1⅜ yards (125.73cm) green solid
- 2⅜ yards (217.17cm) white print for background
- 9 yards (822.96cm) for backing
- ¾ yard (68.58cm) dark blue print for binding

WOF = width of fabric

## CUTTING

Letters in the cutting instructions refer to "shape/size". Keep your cuts organized by letter shape/size and color to make block and quilt assembly easier.

### From the white print, cut:

(18) 9" (22.86cm) squares. Cut twice on the diagonal to make 72 Piece A triangles.

(72) 4¾" (12.07cm) Piece B squares

### From the dark teal solid, cut:

(5) 9" (22.86cm) squares. Cut twice on the diagonal to make 20 Piece A triangles.

(20) 8¼" (20.96cm) Piece C squares

### From the bright teal solid, cut:

(4) 9" (22.86cm) squares. Cut twice on the diagonal to make 16 Piece A triangles.

(16) 8¼" (20.96cm) Piece C squares

### From the green solid, cut:

(18) 9" (22.86cm) squares. Cut twice on the diagonal to make 72 Piece A triangles.

### From the large-scale floral, cut:

(10) 6" (15.24cm) x WOF strips. From EACH strip, cut:
    (2) 6" x 17" (15.24 x 43.18cm) Piece D rectangles
    Trim the remainder of (6) strips to 4¾" (12.07cm).
    From the strips, cut:
    (4) 4¾" (12.07cm) squares. Cut each square on the diagonal to make (12) Piece E triangles.

### From the medium-scale floral print, cut:

(8) 6" (15.24cm) x WOF strips. From EACH strip, cut:
    (2) 6" x 17" (15.24 x 43.18cm) Piece D rectangles
    Trim the remainder of (4) strips to 4¾" (12.07cm).
    From the strips, cut:
    (4) 4¾" (12.07cm) squares. Cut each square on the diagonal to make (8) Piece E triangles.

(16) 6" x 17" (15.24 x 43.18cm) Piece D rectangles

(8) 4¾" (12.07cm) squares. Cut each square in half on the diagonal to make (2) Piece E triangles.

**From the multi white print, cut:**
(5)  6" (15.24) Piece F squares

**From the yellow print, cut:**
(4)  6" (15.24) Piece F squares

**From the dark blue print, cut:**
(10)  2½" (6.35cm) x WOF strips for binding

**From the backing fabric, cut:**
(3)  3 yard (274.32cm) pieces.
     Trim selvedges from the yardage.

## MAKING THE BLOCKS
(9) 32" (81.28CM) FINISHED BLOCKS

1. Draw a diagonal line on the wrong side of
   each 4¾" (12.07cm) Piece B white print
   square. Place a marked square on a Piece C
   dark teal solid square, right sides together,
   aligning raw edges.

2. Trim ¼" (0.64cm) from the sewn line and discard
   the extra triangle. Open and press.

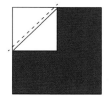

3. Repeat step 2 on the adjacent corner, as shown.
   Make (20) dark teal solid pieced squares.

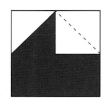 

Make 20

4. Sew a Piece A, dark teal solid triangle to the
   end of the pieced unit, to complete (20) dark
   teal units.

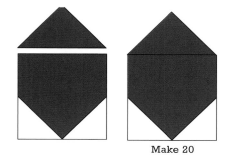

Make 20

5. Repeat steps 1–4, using (16) Piece C, bright teal
   solid squares and 4¾" (12.07cm) Piece B, white
   print squares.

6. Sew a Piece A, bright teal solid triangle to the
   end of the pieced unit. Make (16) bright teal
   solid units.

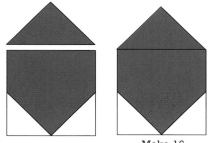

Make 16

### FEARLESS TAKEAWAYS

- When you find a traditional block that seems intimidating, look for seam lines you can eliminate by incorporating stitch-and-flip piecing.

- Mixing solids with prints is an instant update to traditional quilt designs. Add two or three solids so it's clear you made a design decision.

### COLOR LESSON

- The colored triangle point will be slightly more than ¼" (0.64cm) from the edge of the white triangles. This is a deliberate design decision so the pieces will appear to float when the blocks are connected together. It also eliminates the need to have the points match up exactly. "Floating" points is a great technique to alleviate piecing fears.

7. Sew a Piece A green triangle to a Piece A white triangle along the short edge as shown. Make (20) of each.

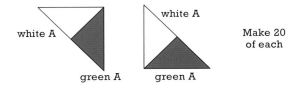

8. Sew the pieced triangles from step 7 to each side of (20) dark teal solid units and (16) bright teal solid units from step 6.

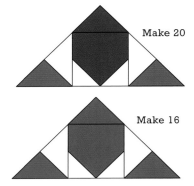

9. Sew (12) dark teal solid and bright teal solids units together.

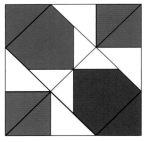

Make 12

10. Sew together (2) large-scale floral Piece E triangles and (2) medium-scale floral Piece E triangles to make a pieced sashing post. Make (4) sashing posts.

Make 4

11. Sew together a Piece E large-scale floral and Piece E medium-scale floral triangle to make a side sashing post. Make (4) of each of the orientations below.

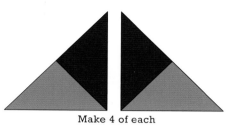

Make 4 of each

## ASSEMBLING THE QUILT TOP

1. Lay out pieces as shown.

2. Starting in the top left corner, sew pieced units together in rows. Sew the rows together to complete the quilt top.

## FINISHING THE QUILT

1. Sew the (3) backing panels together along the long sides. Press seams open.

2. Layer the backing, batting and quilt top. Quilt as desired.

3. Trim the selvedge from each of the binding strips. Sew together using diagonal seams to make one long strip. Press the seams open. Fold the binding in half, wrong sides together, and press along the entire length of the strip. Attach the binding using your preferred method.

**GRIDDED GARDEN**
Finished size: 94" (238.76cm) square

# REVERB

Reverb came about as I sought to make a memory quilt in honor of my father. I wanted a quilt that would remind me of his gentle spirit and softly sparkling blue eyes.

In this quilt, an alternating rotation creates the appearance of a larger star block.

## MODERN

As I experimented with block designs, I kept coming back to the idea that while his memory was softly fading, he would always remain on the edges of my thoughts. Using this concept for design inspiration, I started lightening and removing block elements, creating shadow and ghost blocks. The result is Reverb.

## TRADITIONAL

Traditional pieced chain blocks have been a favorite of quilters for decades because of the potential to alternate rotation of the block and create new designs.

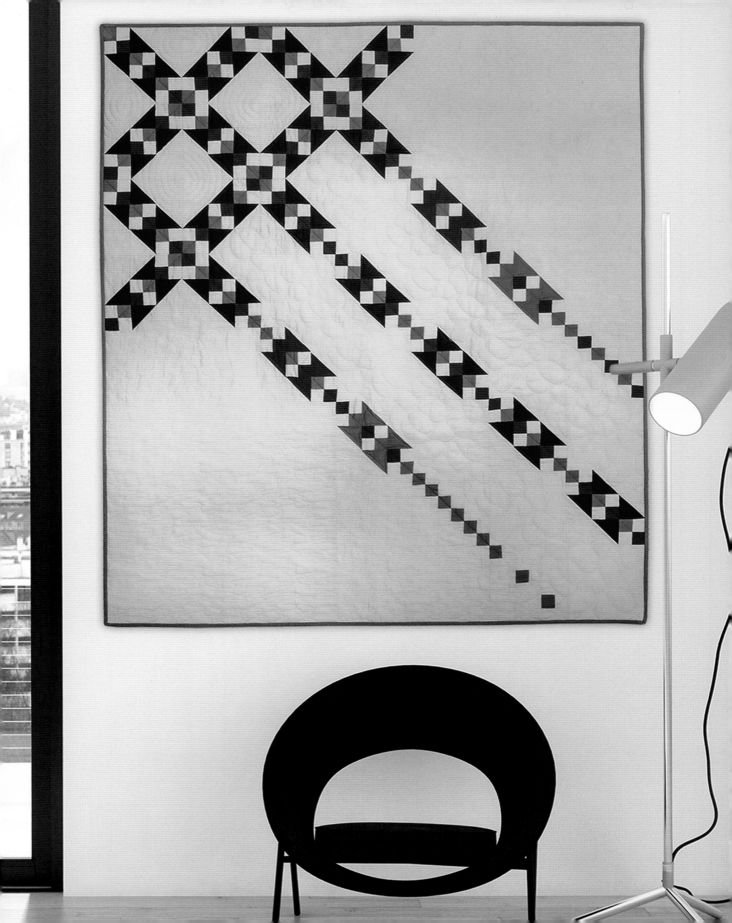

## LEAP OF FAITH

- Ghost elements can also be created by starting out with a complete patchwork block and then replacing one patch at a time with background fabric. If you're unsure about the process, cut out one block using the chosen fabrics and colors, and then cut out an entire block from just the background fabric. Experiment with replacing one patch with the background and take a photo of the resulting block on your phone or camera. Being able to see the resulting block in a small size can help identity strengths and weaknesses of a ghost block.

## COLOR LESSON

- Using a monochromatic color scheme with solid fabrics in shades of a single color is the simplest starting point for block experimentation. When you remove prints from the design equation and focus only on color, it's much easier to see design elements.

## MATERIALS
- 2 yards (182.88cm) pale blue for background and blocks
- ¾ yards (68.58cm) light blue for blocks and binding
- ⅜ yard (34.29cm) medium blue for blocks
- ⅜ yard (34.29cm) dark blue for blocks
- 2⅞ yards (262.89cm) backing fabric

## CUTTING
**From the pale blue, cut:**
- (3) 2⅞" (7.30cm) x WOF strips.
  (42) 2⅞" (7.30cm) squares
- (4) 2½" (6.35cm) x WOF strips. From 3 strips cut,
  (48) 2½" (6.35cm) squares
  From 1 strip, cut:
  (6) 2½" x 4½" (6.35 11.43cm) rectangles
  (3) 1½" x 2½" (3.81 x 6.35cm) rectangles
- (5) 6½" (16.51cm) x WOF strips.
  From (1) strip, cut:
  (1) 6½" x 30½" (16.51 x 77.47cm) rectangle
  (1) 6½" (16.51cm) squares
  From (1) strip, cut:
  (1) 6½" x 24½" (16.51 x 62.23cm) rectangles
  (3) 6½" (16.51cm) squares
  From (1) strip cut:
  (2) 6½" x 18½" (16.51 x 46.99cm) rectangles
  From 1 strip, cut:
  (1) 6½" x 18½" (16.51 x 46.99cm) rectangles
  (3) 6½" (16.51cm) squares
  From (1) strip, cut:
  (2) 6½" x 12½" (16.51 x 31.75cm) rectangles
  (3) 6½" (16.51cm) squares

**From the light blue, cut:**
- (4) 2⅞" (7.30cm) squares
- (5) 2½" (6.35cm) x WOF strips for binding
- (3) 1½" (3.81cm) x WOF strips

**From the medium blue, cut:**
- (4) 2⅞" (7.30cm) squares
- (3) 1½" (3.81cm) x WOF strips

**From the dark blue, cut:**
- (34) 2⅞" (7.30cm) squares

## MAKING THE "A" BLOCKS
6" (15.24CM) FINISHED BLOCKS

*Note: There are (3) "A" blocks. Label each one with letter/ number after sewing.*

1. Draw a diagonal line on the wrong side of (34) 2⅞" (7.30cm) pale blue squares.
2. Pin (1) marked pale blue square, right sides together, on (1) 2⅞" (7.30cm) dark blue square. Sew ¼" (0.64cm) away on both sides of the drawn line.

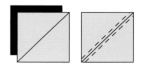

3. Cut the square in half diagonally on the drawn line. Press the seam toward the dark blue triangle and trim, if necessary, to measure 2½" (6.35cm) square. Make a total of (68) pale/dark blue half-square triangle units.

Make 68

4. Using the remaining (8) pale blue squares, (4) 2⅞" (7.30cm) medium blue squares and (4) 2⅞" (7.30cm) light blue squares, repeat steps 1–3 to make a total of (8) 2½" (6.35cm) pale/medium blue and (8) 2½" (6.35cm) pale/light half-square triangle units.

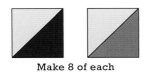

Make 8 of each

5. Sew (1) 1½" (3.81cm) x WOF pale blue strip to (1) 1½" (3.81cm) light blue strip to make a two-strip panel. Press the seam toward the light blue strip. Make (3) panels.

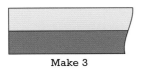

Make 3

6. Cross-cut the (2) strip panels into 1½" (3.81cm) sections. Cut a total of (75) 1½" x 2½" (3.81 x 6.35cm) pale/light blue units. Set aside (9) units to use in making Block B.

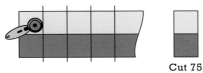

Cut 75

7. Sew (1) 1½" (3.81cm) x WOF pale blue strip to (1) 1½" (3.81cm) medium blue strip to make a two-strip panel. Press the seam toward the medium blue strip. Make (3) panels.

Make 3

8. Cross-cut the two-strip panels into 1½" (3.81cm) units. Cut a total of (66) 1½" x 2½" (3.81 x 6.35cm) pale/medium blue units.

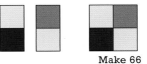

Cut 66

9. Sew (1) pale/medium blue unit to (1) pale/light blue unit, as shown. Press seam toward the pale/medium blue unit to make a 2½" (6.35cm) light/medium blue four-patch square. Make (66) squares. Set aside (3) four-patch squares to use in the B blocks.

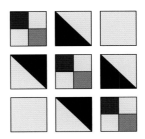

Make 66

10. Lay out (4) pale/dark blue half-square triangles, (3) light/medium blue four-patch squares and (2) 2½" (6.35cm) light blue squares in three rows of three squares each, noting the orientation of each square.

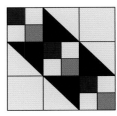

11. Sew the squares together in each row. Press seams toward the half-square triangle units. Join the rows. Press the seams in one direction to make a 6½" (16.51cm) Block A-1. Make (17) blocks.

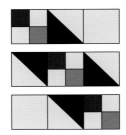

Make 17

## FEARLESS TAKEAWAYS

- Any block can be updated with ghost elements. By highlighting or minimizing a block element, new shapes can emerge which create an entirely new focus.

## CONFIDENCE BOOSTER

- Varying both the color progression of prints and the value progression of background fabrics adds visual complexity to a simple pieced block.

## ALTERNATIVE COLORWAY

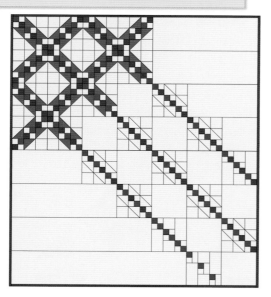

12. Repeat steps 10 and 11, laying out (4) pale/medium blue half-square triangles, (3) light/medium blue four-patch squares and (2) 2½" (6.35cm) light blue squares, noting the orientation of each square.

13. Sew the squares together in each row. Press seam toward the half-square triangle units. Join the rows. Press the seams in one direction to make a 6½" (16.51cm) Block A-2. Make (2) blocks.

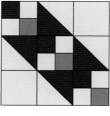

**Make 2**

14. Repeat steps 10 and 11, laying out (4) pale/light blue half-square triangles, (3) light/medium blue four-patch squares and (2) 2½" (6.35cm) light blue squares, noting the orientation of each square.

15. Sew the squares together in each row. Press seam toward the half-square triangle units. Join the rows. Press the seams in one direction to make a 6½" (16.51cm) Block A-3. Make (2) blocks.

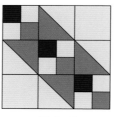

**Make 2**

# MAKING THE "B" BLOCKS

***Note: There are (3) "B" blocks. Label each one with letter/number after sewing.***

1. Using the extra (3) light/medium blue four-patch squares from step 9 of Block A, sew (1) four-patch square to the top of (1) 2½" x 4½" (6.35 11.43cm) pale blue rectangle, as shown. Press seam toward the rectangle to make a side block. Make (2) side blocks.

Make 2

2. Sew (1) four-patch square between (2) 2½" (6.35cm) pale blue squares. Press seams toward the squares to make a middle block. Make (1) middle block.

Make 1

3. Sew the middle block from step 2 between the (2) side blocks, as shown. Press seams toward the side block to make a 6½" (16.51cm) Block B-1. Make (1) block.

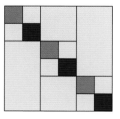

Make 1

4. Using (6) of the pale/light blue units from step 6 of Block A, sew (2) sections together as shown. Press seam toward one pale/light blue section to make a 2½" (6.35cm) light blue four-patch square. Make (3) four-patch squares.

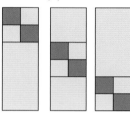

Make 3

5. Repeat steps 1–3, using (3) four-patch squares, (2) 2½" x 4½" (6.35 11.43cm) pale blue rectangles and (2) 2½" (6.35cm) pale blue squares to make a 6½" (16.51cm) Block B-2. Make (1) block.

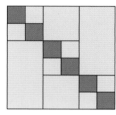

Make 1

6. Using the remaining (3) pale/light blue sections set aside in step 6 of Block A, sew (1) section to the right side of (1) 1½" x 2½" (3.81 x 6.35cm) pale blue rectangle. Press seam toward the rectangle to make a 2½" (6.35cm) light blue three-patch square. Make (3) three-patch squares.

Make 3

7. Repeat steps 1–3, using (3) three-patch squares, (2) 2½" x 4½" (6.35cm x 11.43cm) pale blue rectangles and (2) 2½" (6.35cm) pale blue squares to make a 6½" (16.51cm) Block B-3. Make (1) block.

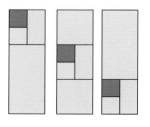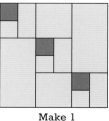

Make 1

## ASSEMBLING THE QUILT

1. Referring to the Quilt Assembly Diagram, lay out the A blocks, the B blocks, (9) 6½" (16.51cm) pale blue squares and the (7) large pale blue rectangles of various lengths in eight rows, as shown, noting the orientation of each block.

2. Sew the blocks, squares and rectangles together in each row. Press the seams in rows 1, 3, 5 and 7 to the right. Press the seams in rows 2, 4, 6 and 8 to the left.

3. Join the rows. Press the seams in one direction to complete a 42½" x 48½" (107.95 x 123.19cm) unfinished quilt top.

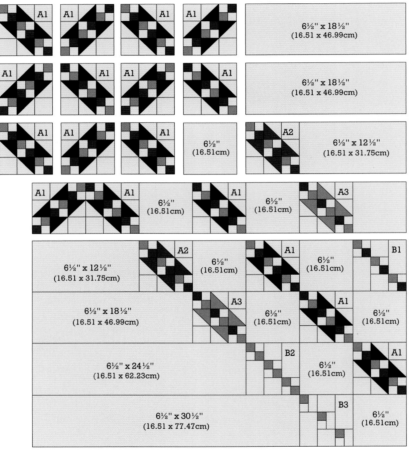

**Quilt Assembly Diagram**

## FINISHING THE QUILT

1. Cut the backing yardage into (2) yards (182.88cm) x WOF pieces. Trim the selvedges. Piece the (2) panels together along the long edge, using a ½" (1.27cm) seam, to make the backing.

2. Layer the quilt top, backing and batting. Quilt as desired.

3. Trim the selvedge from each of the (5) binding strips. Sew together using diagonal seams to make one long strip. Press the seams open. Fold the binding in half, wrong sides together, and press along the entire length of the strip. Attach the binding using your preferred method.

# TILTAWHIRL

Starting with a group of traditional patchwork units and arranging them in unusual ways can lead to fun, modern blocks.

Using these two units in a four-patch block layout instead of a traditional nine-patch layout immediately disrupted the expected block grid and dynamics.

## MODERN

For Tiltawhirl, I started with a half-square triangle unit and a "peaky and spike" triangle unit, which is composed of a center triangle and two long, skinny triangles.

By coloring the patches so the two triangle shapes appear to be one unit, the block appears to have an unusual shape that can actually be achieved with traditional rotary cutting.

Adding a narrow sashing between each block opened up the design and let the pinwheel shapes really sparkle.

## TRADITIONAL

When traditional blocks are set side by side, the resulting quilt has an interesting pinwheel dynamic but is somewhat busy and has little resting place for the eyes.

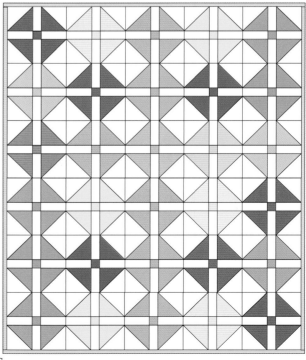

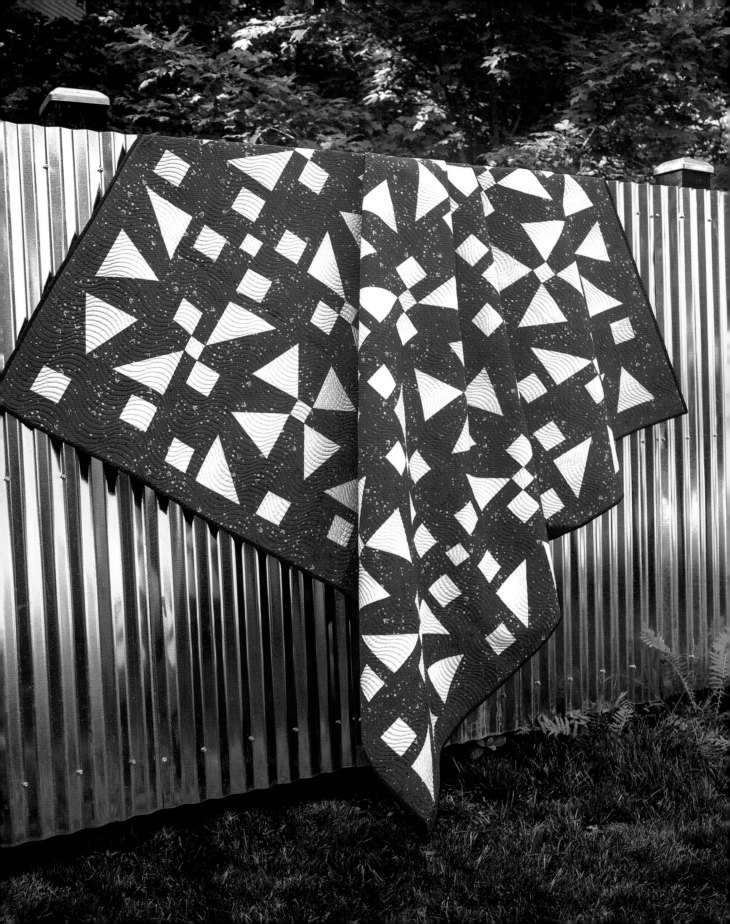

## FEARLESS TAKEAWAYS

- Consider using fabrics in unexpected ways—placing prints next to each other instead of interrupting patches with background can lead to unique shapes.

## CONFIDENCE BOOSTER

- Because this block features triangle shapes you may not have sewn before, consider cutting out a test block and piecing before cutting everything. For maximum accuracy, I often mark dots where the angles of lines intersect, and then pin those dots and use them as reference points when joining seams. Acrylic templates are available to aid with this method.

- **PRO TIP:** Use the included templates (see pages 120–125) to cut Pieces B and C or, alternatively, use a Tri Recs ruler. Keep pieces organized by color and template shape.

MATERIALS
- 2½ yards (228.60cm) white tonal print
- 6¼ yards (571.50cm) purple print
- ¾ yard (68.58cm) dark purple print for binding
- 9 yards (822.96cm) for backing

WOF = width of fabric

## CUTTING

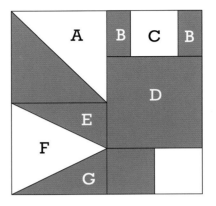

**From the white print, cut:**
(4)  6⅞" (17.46cm) x WOF strips. From the strips, cut: (21) 6⅞" (17.46cm) squares. Cut in half on the diagonal to make (42) Piece A triangles.
(7)  3½" (8.89cm) x WOF strips. From the strips, cut: (84) 3½" (8.89cm) Piece C squares

**From the purple print, cut:**
(4)  6⅞" (17.46cm) x WOF strips. From the strips, cut: (21) 66⅞" (17.46cm) squares. Cut in half on the diagonal to make (42) Piece A triangles.
(7)  2" (5.08cm) x WOF strips. From the strips, cut: (84) 2" x 3½" (5.08 x 8.89cm) Piece B rectangles.
(7)  6½" (16.51cm) x WOF strips. From the strips, cut: (42) 6½" (16.51cm) Piece D squares.
(42) Piece E triangles using the template shown on page 124
(42) Piece G triangles using the template shown on page 125
(24) 2½" (6.35cm) x WOF strips. Cut into (71) 2½" x 12½" (6.35 x 31.75cm) sashing strips.
(10) 3½" (8.89cm) x WOF strips. Piece the strips together along the short edge. Cut into (2) 3½" x 88½" (8.89 x 224.79cm) top/bottom border strips, and (2) 3½" x 96½" (8.89 x 245.11cm) side border strips.

**From the dark purple print, cut:**
(10) 2½" (6.35cm) x WOF strips for binding.

## MAKING THE BLOCKS
(42) 12" (30.48CM) FINISHED BLOCKS

1. Sew a Piece A purple and white triangle together along the long edge using a ¼" (0.64cm) seam. Press toward the purple print. Repeat to make (42) half-square triangles.

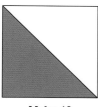

**Make 42**

2. Sew a Piece C purple square to a Piece C white square. Repeat to make (42) pieced rectangles.

**Make 42**

3. Sew a Piece B purple rectangle to each side of a Piece C white square. Repeat to make (42) pieced units.

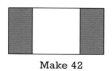

**Make 42**

4. Sew a Piece E and G triangle to the long edges of a Piece F triangle, paying attention to orientation. Press seams toward the purple print. Repeat to make (42) units.

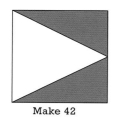

**Make 42**

5. Sew the two pieced rectangle units from steps 2–3, to opposite sides of a Piece D square. Make (42) rectangle units.

**Make 42**

6. Sew the HST units from step 1 to the triangle units from step 4, paying attention to orientation. Make (42) rectangles.

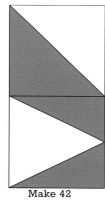

**Make 42**

7. Referring to the illustration below, sew together the units from steps 5–6 to make (42) 12½" (31.75cm) unfinished block units.

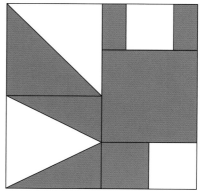

**Make 42**

ASSEMBLING THE QUILT

1. Referring to the illustration, orient (6) of the blocks and sew them together, alternating with a 2½" x 12½" (6.35 x 31.75cm) sashing strip between each block. Make (4) "odd" rows.

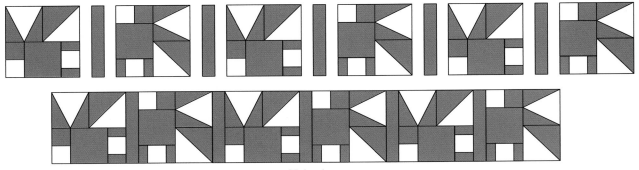

**Make 4**

2. Referring to the illustration, Make (3) "even" rows.

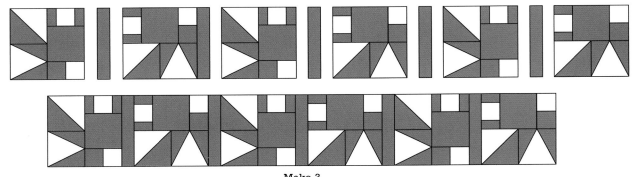

**Make 3**

3. Sew (6) 2½" x 12½" (6.35 x 31.75cm) sashing strips, alternating with 2½" (6.35cm) squares, as shown. Make (5) sashing strips.

**Make 5**

4. Starting with an "odd" row from step 1, sew the rows, alternating with the "even" rows from step 2. Sew a sashing strip from step 3 between each row.

5. Sew a 3½" x 88½" (8.89 x 224.79cm) border strip to the top and bottom of the quilt. Sew a 3½" x 96½" (8.89 x 245.11cm) border strip to each long edge of the quilt.

## FINISHING THE QUILT

1. Cut the backing yardage into (3) pieces, each 3 yards (274.32cm) x WOF. Trim the selvedges from the yardage.

2. Piece the (3) panels together along the long edge to make the backing.

3. Layer the quilt top, backing and batting. Quilt as desired.

4. Trim the selvedge from each of the (10) binding strips. Sew together using diagonal seams to make one long strip. Press the seams open. Fold the binding in half, wrong sides together, and press along the entire length of the strip. Attach the binding using your preferred method.

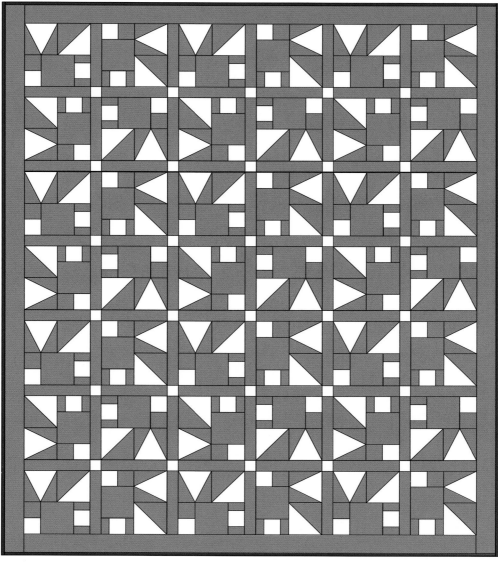

**TILTAWHIRL**
Finished size: 88" x 102" (223.52 x 259.08cm)

## LEAP OF FAITH

- To make experimenting with new arrangements for traditional block patches easier, start with only two fabrics that contrast with each other. Having just two colors interacting allows new shapes to emerge more easily.

- Take this concept one step further by randomly placing traditional shapes into unusual layouts. This block becomes this quilt when set side by side.

- Look at the magic that happens when you add simple sashing with a cornerstone—a very traditional element that quilters are familiar with.

## ALTERNATIVE COLORWAY

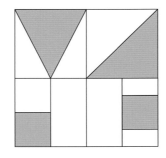

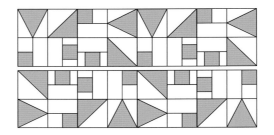

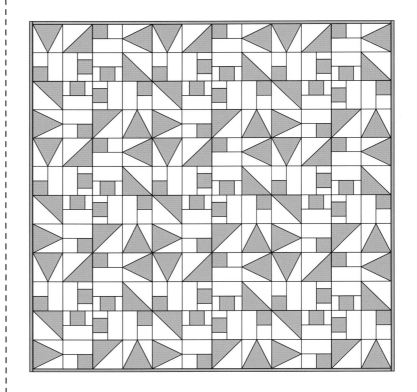

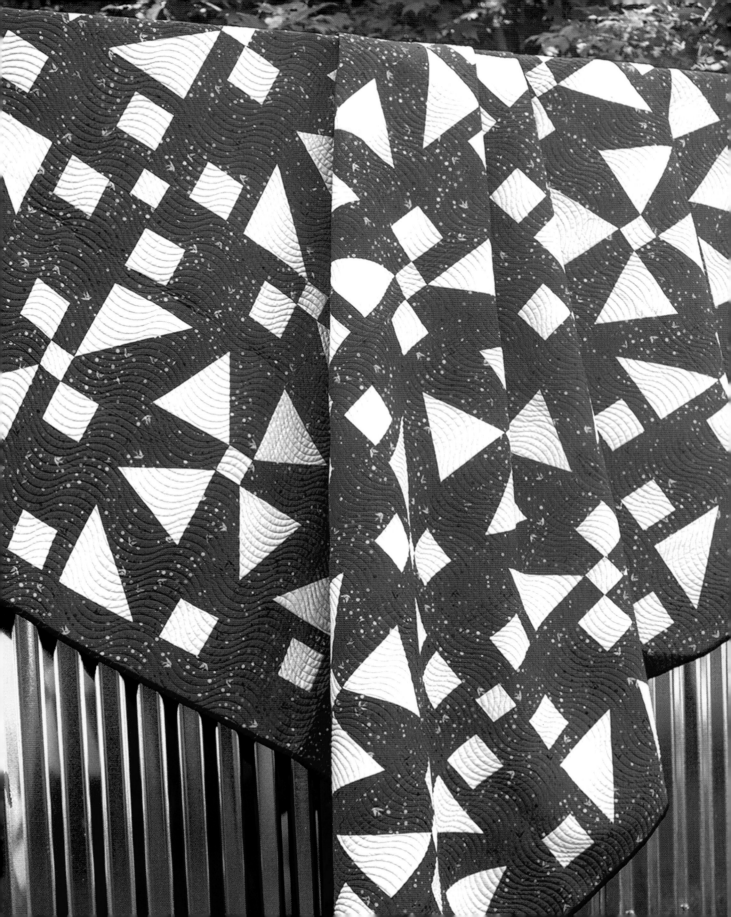

# Tiltawhirl Templates

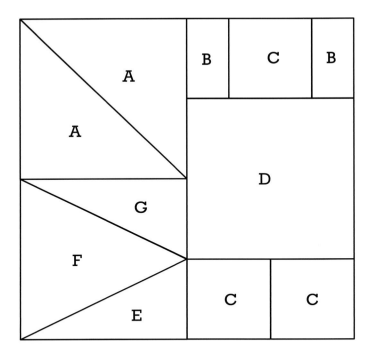

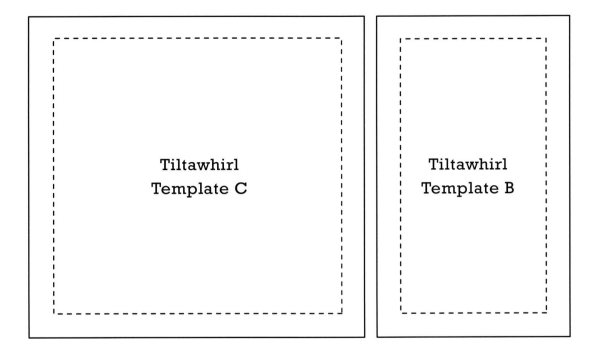

Tiltawhirl
Template C

Tiltawhirl
Template B

# Tiltawhirl Templates

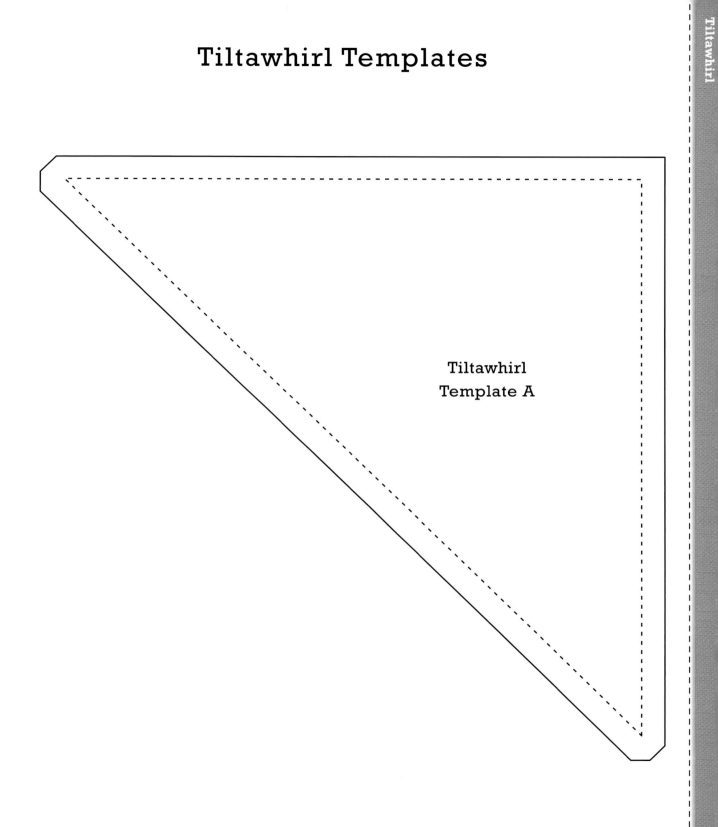

Tiltawhirl
Template A

# Tiltawhirl Templates

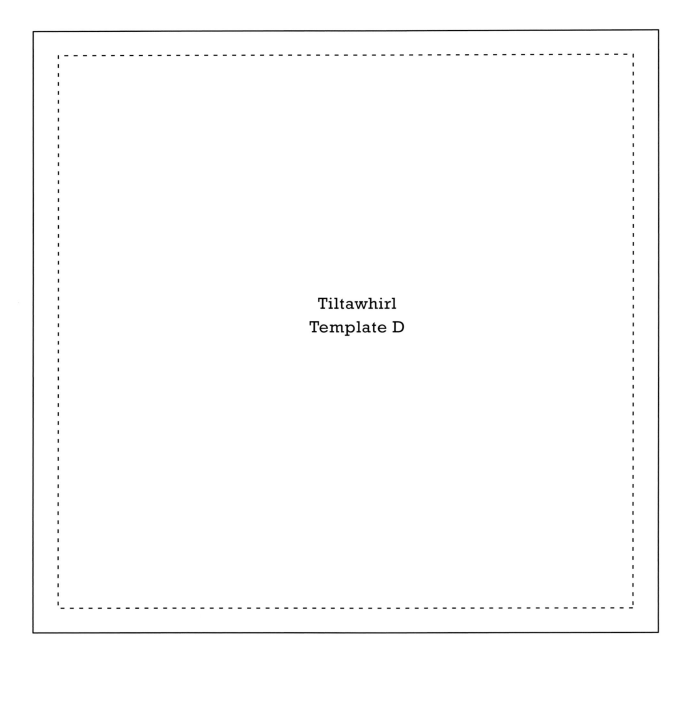

Tiltawhirl
Template D

# Tiltawhirl Templates

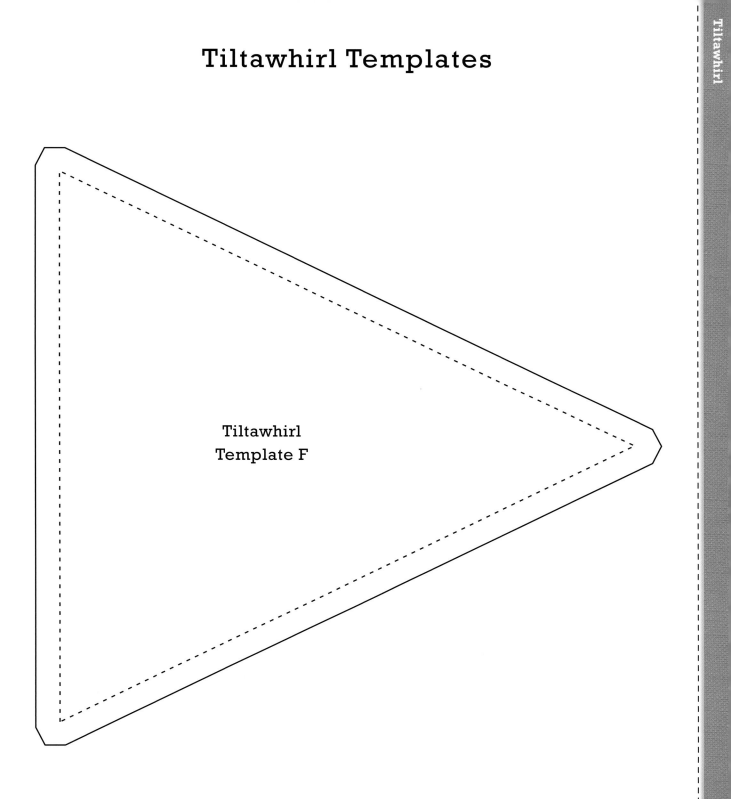

Tiltawhirl
Template F

# Tiltawhirl Templates

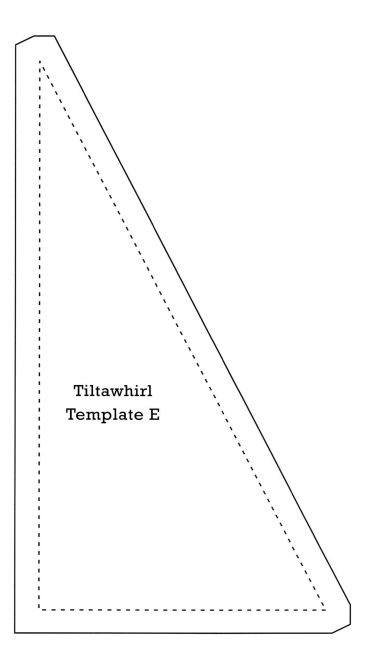

Tiltawhirl
Template E

# Tiltawhirl Templates

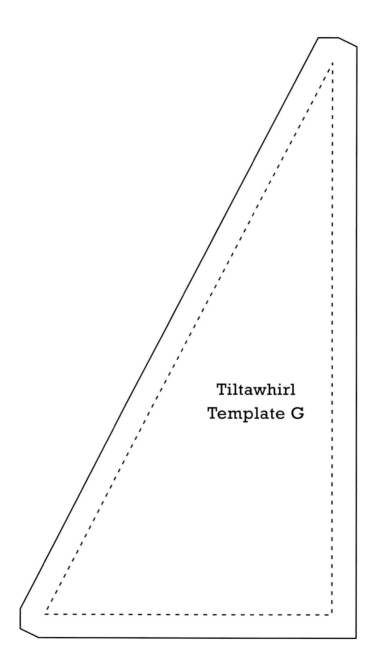

Tiltawhirl
Template G

# WANDERING RIVER

After I finalized my River Falls batik collection, I knew I wanted to create a quilt based on a traditional block that had a modern feel and included the batiks.

By combining two sizes of the block within the quilt, a more dynamic layout emerged.

## MODERN

I love working with batik fabrics but find quilters often avoid them.

The Drunkard's Path block appealed to me because so many shapes could be created depending on how the quarter circles were rotated and placed to create partial circles.

## TRADITIONAL

The Drunkard's Path is a classic that has go-to setting options.

## LEAP OF FAITH

- Experiment with placing various sizes of a single block within a quilt to create interest.

- The easiest way to make sure your blocks will fit together is to either multiply the size of the starting block by two or three, so your initial block will fit next to the larger block in equal units. You could also divide the size of your starting block by a number that results in a logical result that can be achieved with standard rotary cutting.

## MATERIALS

- ⅛ yard (11.43cm) dark purple Fabric 14
- ¼ yard (22.86cm) EACH of (2) medium purples Fabrics 3 and 5
- ½ yard (45.72cm) medium blue Fabric 4
- ⅛ yard (11.43cm) dark blue Fabric 9
- ⅜ yard (34.30cm) second dark blue Fabric 6
- 1⅛ yards (102.87cm) multi-color Fabric 7 print for blocks and binding.
- ⅛ yard (11.43cm) (11.43cm) bright green Fabric 13
- ¼ yard (22.86cm) second bright green Fabric 15
- ¼ yard (22.86cm) medium green Fabric 18
- ⅜ yard (34.30cm) earthy green Fabric 5
- ¼ yard (22.86cm) EACH of (2) browns Fabrics 16 and 17
- ⅝ yard (57.15cm) EACH of (2) neutral backgrounds Fabrics 1 and 2
- ½ yard (45.72cm) of a neutral background Fabric 11
- 1⅛ yards (102.87cm) of a neutral background Fabric 10
- 1½ yards (137.16cm) of a neutral background Fabric 8
- ½ yard (411.48cm) for backing

## COLOR LESSON

- This fabric key makes it easier to understand the color and value relationships, and relates to the written instructions in terms of what fabric goes where.

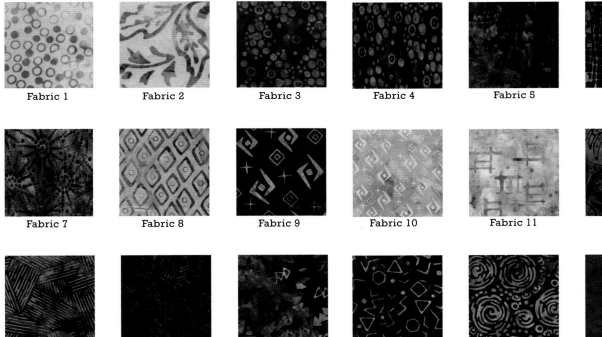

Fabric 1    Fabric 2    Fabric 3    Fabric 4    Fabric 5    Fabric 6

Fabric 7    Fabric 8    Fabric 9    Fabric 10    Fabric 11    Fabric 12

Fabric 13    Fabric 14    Fabric 15    Fabric 16    Fabric 17    Fabric 18

*Featuring River Falls batiks by Sarah Maxwell*

# CUTTING
GENERAL TEMPLATE CUTTING DIAGRAMS

*Use templates to cut fabric as shown, unless otherwise instructed. Keeping fabric organized by fabric number and size will make piecing easier.*

**From Fabric 1, cut:**
(4)  5" (12.70cm) x WOF strips. From the strips, cut: (32) of Template A, as shown.

**From Fabric 2, cut:**
(4)  5" (12.7cm) x WOF strips. From the strips, cut: (32) of Template A, as shown.

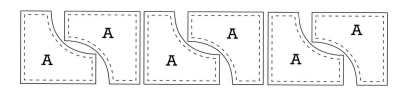

**From Fabric 3, cut:**
(2)  3½" (8.89cm) x WOF strips. From the strips, cut: (14) of Template B, as shown.

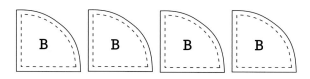

**From Fabric 4, cut:**
(2)  6½" (16.51cm) x WOF strips. From the strips, cut: (10) of Template D, as shown.

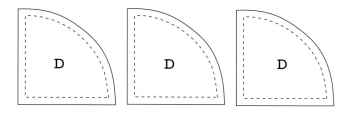

**From Fabric 5, cut:**
(1)  3½" (8.89cm) x WOF strips. From the strips, cut: (32) of Template B, as shown.

**From Fabric 6, cut:**
(3)  3½" (8.89cm) x WOF strips. From the strips, cut: (24) of Template B, as shown.

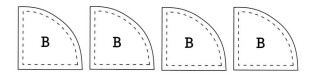

# PROJECTS

## FEARLESS TAKEAWAYS

- Classic Drunkard's Path setting options: By adding a single, small additional pieced element in one position and subtracting some of the blocks, the block is instantly modern.

- Watch what happens when a simple rectangle is added to the block and more plain blocks are added to the design.

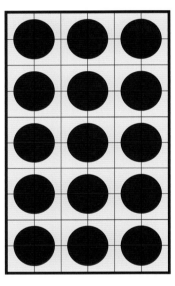

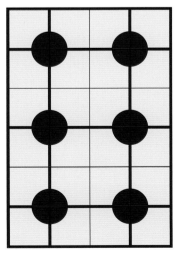

**From Fabric 7, cut:**
(2)  6½" (16.51cm) x WOF strips.
     From the strips, cut:
     (10) of Template D, as shown.
(8)  2½" (6.35cm) x WOF strips for binding

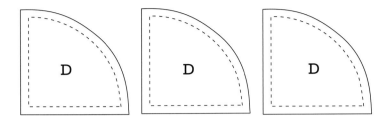

**From Fabric 8, (directional print), cut:**
(2)  5" (12.7cm) x WOF strips. From the strips, cut:
     (14) of Template A, as shown.

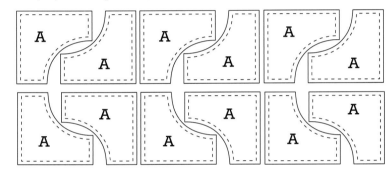

(4)  9½" (24.13cm) x WOF strips.
     From the strips, cut:
     (10) of Template C, as shown.

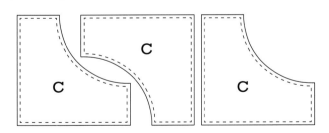

**From Fabric 9, (directional print), cut:**
(1)  3½" (8.89cm) x WOF strip. From the strip, cut:
(4)  of Template B, and (4) of Template B reversed, as shown.

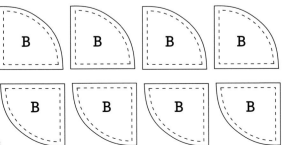

**From Fabric 10, (directional print), cut:**

(7) 5" (12.7cm) x WOF strips. From the strips, cut: (44) of Template A, as shown.

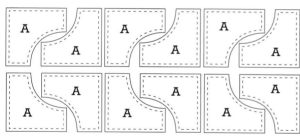

**From Fabric 11, cut:**

(3) 5" (12.7cm) x WOF strips. From the strips, cut: (28) of Template A, as shown.

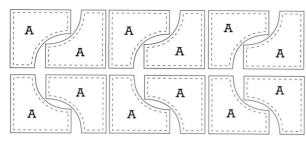

**From Fabric 12, cut:**

(2) 3½" (8.89cm) x WOF strips. From the strips, cut: (22) of Template B, as shown.

**From Fabric 13, cut:**

(1) 3½" (8.89cm) x WOF strip. From the strip, cut: (2) of Template B, as shown.

**From Fabric 14, cut:**

(1) 3½" (8.89cm) x WOF strip. From the strip, cut: (8) of Template B, as shown.

**From Fabric 15, cut:**

(2) 3½" (8.89cm) x WOF strips. From the strips, cut: (16) of Template B, as shown.

**From Fabric 16, cut:**

(2) 3½" (8.89cm) x WOF strips. From the strips, cut: (18) of Template B, as shown.

**From Fabric 17, cut:**

(2) 3½" (8.89cm) x WOF strips. From the strips, cut: (18) of Template B, as shown.

**From Fabric 18, cut:**

(2) 3½" (8.89cm) x WOF strips. From the strips, cut: (14) of Template B, as shown.

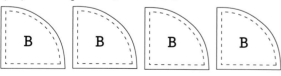

## MAKING THE DRUNKARD PATH BLOCKS

9" (22.86CM) SQUARE AND 4½" (11.43CM)" SQUARE FINISHED BLOCK SIZES

*NOTE: The following method, or your preferred curved piecing method, can be used to make the blocks.*

1. Place a Fabric 13 Template B unit on top of a Fabric 2 Template A unit, right sides together, matching the straight edges of the B unit to the straight edges of the A unit. Starting in the center of the curves, pin together, easing the fabrics along the edges, being careful not to stretch the curves.

2. Using the glue marker, begin on the right side and dab a little glue inside the seam allowance of the A unit. Press the B unit onto the glue. Continue in the same way until you reach the left side of the curve.

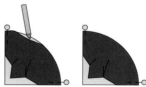

3. With the B unit on top, and starting on the left edge, sew the pieces together using a ¼" (0.64cm) seam allowance. Use the flat side of the curved tip of That Purple Thang tool to smooth out any wrinkles in front of the needle.

4. Press the seam allowance toward the B unit. Make (2)* fabric 2 and 13 units. (*Note: these units are included in the chart that follows.)

5. Repeat steps 1–4 and sew each pair of A/B units together to make a total of (176) 5" (12.7cm) square Drunkard Path blocks in the following fabric combinations.

| Sew Temp A Fabric # | Sew Temp B Fabric # | And make this many |
|---|---|---|
| 1 | 17 | 18 |
| 1 | 18 | 14 |
| 2 | 3 | 10 |
| 2 | 12 | 4 |
| 2 | 13 | *2 |
| 2 | 15 | 16 |
| **8 | 3 | 4 |
| **8 | 12 | 10 |
| **10 | 5 | 32 |
| **10 | 6 | 12 |
| **10 | **9 | 8 |
| **10 | 16 | 18 |
| 11 | 6 | 12 |
| 11 | 12 | 8 |
| 11 | 14 | 8 |

** Directional print. Note the orientation before piecing.

6. Repeat steps 1–4 and sew each pair of C/D units together to make a total of (20) 9½" (24.13cm) square Drunkard Path blocks in the following fabric combinations.

| Sew Temp C Fabric # | Sew Temp D Fabric # | And make this many |
|---|---|---|
| **8 | 4 | 10 |
| **8 | 7 | 10 |

## ASSEMBLING THE QUILT TOP

1. Lay out (2) 5" (12.7cm) fabric 2 and 13, (2) fabric 2 and 15, (8) fabric 10 and 9, (8) fabric 11 and 12, (8) fabric 11 and 14, (18) fabric 1 and 17 and (18) fabric 10 and 16 squares in eight rows of eight squares each, noting the placement and orientation of each square.

2. Sew the squares together in rows. Press the seams in rows 1, 3, 5 and 7 to the right. Press the seams in rows 2, 4, 6 and 8 to the left.

3. Sew the rows together to make a 36½" (92.71cm) center section. Press the seams in one direction.

4. Sew (2) 9½" (24.13cm) fabric 8 and 4 squares, alternating with (2) 9½" (24.13cm) fabric 8 and 7 square, as shown. Press the seams in one direction to make a side panel. Make (2). Sew the side panels to opposite sides of the center section, noting the orientation of each side panel.

5. Sew (3) 9½" (24.13cm) fabric 8 and 4 squares, alternating with (3) 9½" (24.13cm) fabric 8 and 7 squares, as shown. Press the seams in one direction to make a top/bottom panel. Make (2). Sew the top/bottom panels to the remaining sides of the center section, noting the orientation of each top/bottom panel to make a 54½" (138.43cm) quilt top.

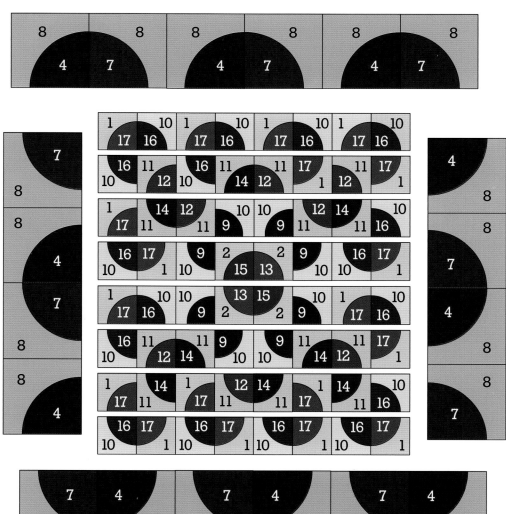

6. Sew (2) 5" (12.7cm) fabric 11 and 6 squares together, as shown. Press the seam in one direction. Make (6) fabric 11 and 6 panels.

**Make 6**
**11-6 panels**

7. Sew (2) 5" (12.7cm) fabric 10 and 6 squares together, as shown. Press the seam in one direction. Make (6) fabric 10 and 6 panels.

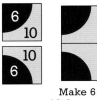

**Make 6**
**10-6 panels**

8. Sew (1) 5" (12.7cm) fabric 2 and 3 square to (1) 5" (12.7cm) fabric 8 and 12 square, as shown. Press the seam in one direction. Make (8) for the top/bottom panels.

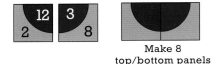

**Make 8**
**top/bottom panels**

9. Sew (1) 5" (12.7cm) fabric 2 and 12 square to (1) (1) 5" (12.7cm) fabric 8 and 3 square, as shown. Press the seam in one direction. Make (4) for the side panels.

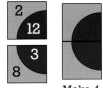

**Make 4**
**side panels**

10. Sew (3) fabric 10 and 6 panels, alternating with (2) side panels, as shown. Press the seams in one direction. Sew a fabric 8 and 12 square to the left end and sew fabric 2 and 3 square to the right end to make a side border. Make (2). Referring to the Border Diagram on page 135, sew to the opposite sides of the center section unit.

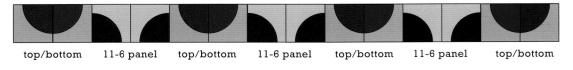

12-8    10-6 panel    side    10-6 panel    side    10-6 panel    3-2

11  Sew (4) top/bottom panels, alternating with (3) fabric 11 and 6 panels, as shown. Press the seam in one direction to make a top/bottom border. Make 2. Referring to the Border Diagram on page 135, sew to the top and bottom of the center section unit.

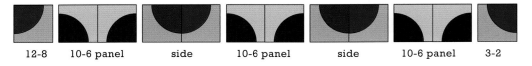

top/bottom    11-6 panel    top/bottom    11-6 panel    top/bottom    11-6 panel    top/bottom

**Border Diagram**

12. Sew (2) 5" (12.7cm) fabric 10 and 5 squares together, as shown. Press the seams in one direction. Make (16) total fabric 10 and 5 panels.

**Make 8**

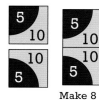

**Make 8**

13. Sew (1) 5" (12.7cm) fabric 1 and 18 square to (1) 5" (12.7cm) fabric 2 and 15 square, as shown. Press the seam in one direction. Make (12) total border panels.

**Make6**

**Make 6**

14. Sew (4) fabric 10 and 5 panels, alternating with (3) border panels, as shown. Press the seams in one direction to make a border. Make (4). Sew (2) borders to the sides of the center section, noting the orientation of the border panels. Press the seams toward the border panels.

| 10-5 panel | Border panel | 10-5 panel | Border panel | 10-5 panel | Border panel | 10-5 panel |

15. Sew a fabric 2 and 15 square to the left end of (1) remaining border from step 14. Sew a fabric 1 and 18 square to the right end of the border to make a top/bottom border. Make (2). Sew to the top and bottom of the center section unit to complete the quilt top.

# FINISHING THE QUILT

1. Cut the backing yardage into (2) 2¼ yards (205.74cm) x WOF pieces. Trim the selvedges. Piece the (2) panels together along the long edge, using a ½" (1/27cm) seam, to make the backing.

2. Layer the quilt top, backing and batting. Quilt as desired.

3. Trim the selvedge from each of the (8) binding strips. Sew together using diagonal seams to make one long strip. Press the seams open. Fold the binding in half, wrong sides together, and press along the entire length of the strip. Attach the binding using your preferred method.

**WANDERING RIVER**
Finished 72" x 72" (182.88 x 182.88cm)

# Wandering River Templates

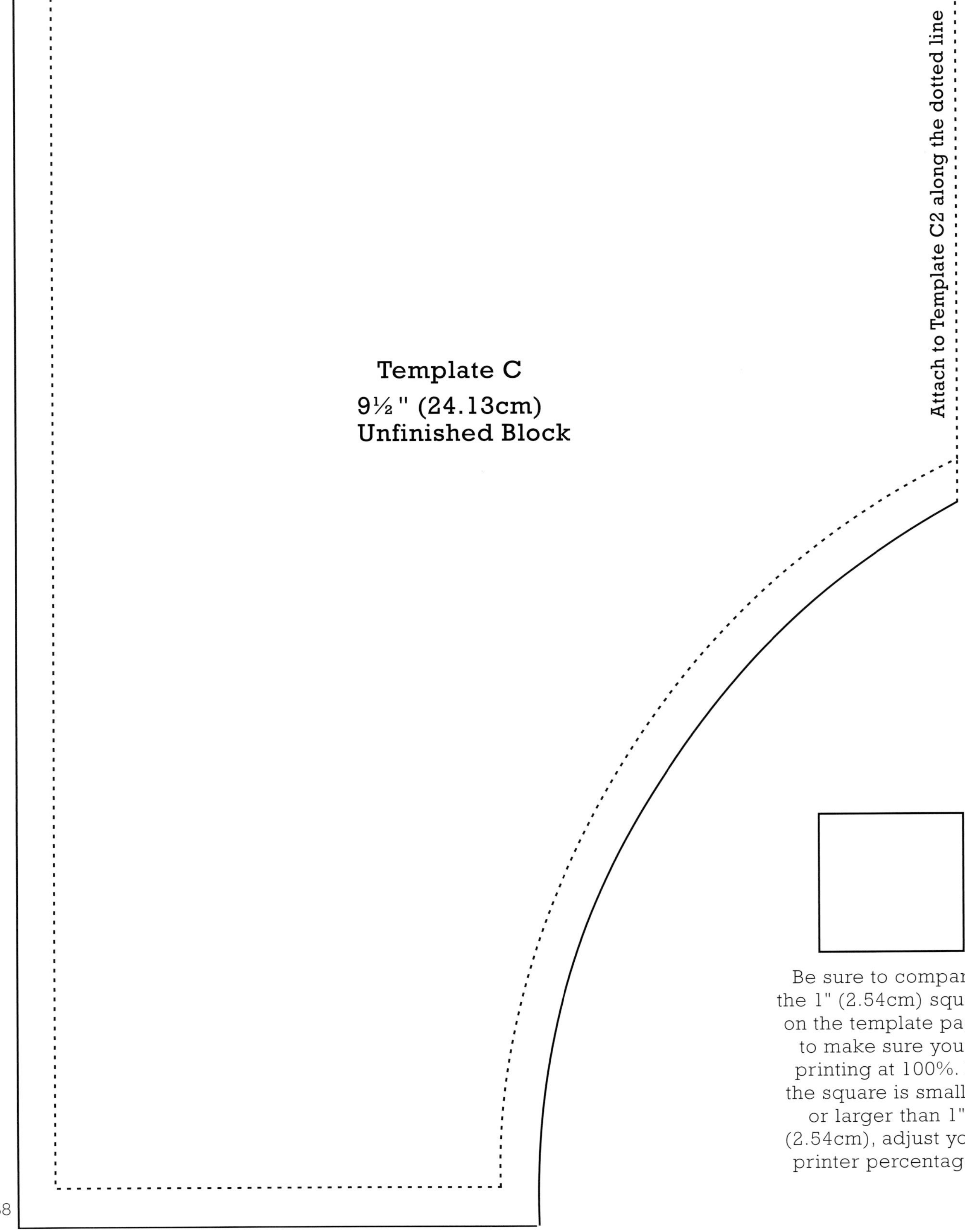

**Template C**
**9½" (24.13cm)**
**Unfinished Block**

Attach to Template C2 along the dotted line

Be sure to compare the 1" (2.54cm) square on the template page to make sure your printing at 100%. If the square is smaller or larger than 1" (2.54cm), adjust your printer percentage.

# Wandering River Templates

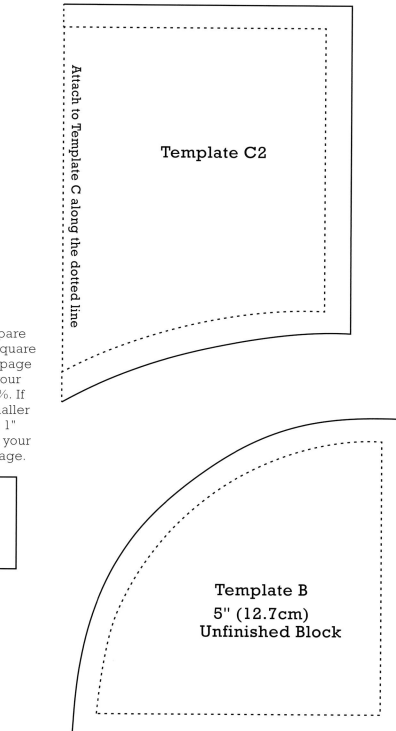

Template C2

Attach to Template C along the dotted line

Be sure to compare the 1" (2.54cm) square on the template page to make sure your printing at 100%. If the square is smaller or larger than 1" (2.54cm), adjust your printer percentage.

Template B
5" (12.7cm)
Unfinished Block

# Wandering River Templates

Be sure to compare the 1" (2.54cm) square on the template page to make sure your printing at 100%. If the square is smaller or larger than 1" (2.54cm), adjust your printer percentage.

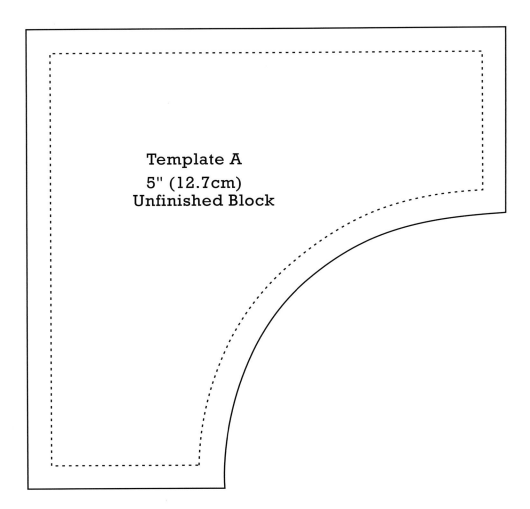

**Template A**
**5" (12.7cm)**
**Unfinished Block**

# Wandering River Templates

Be sure to compare the 1" (2.54cm) square on the template page to make sure your printing at 100%. If the square is smaller or larger than 1" (2.54cm), adjust your printer percentage.

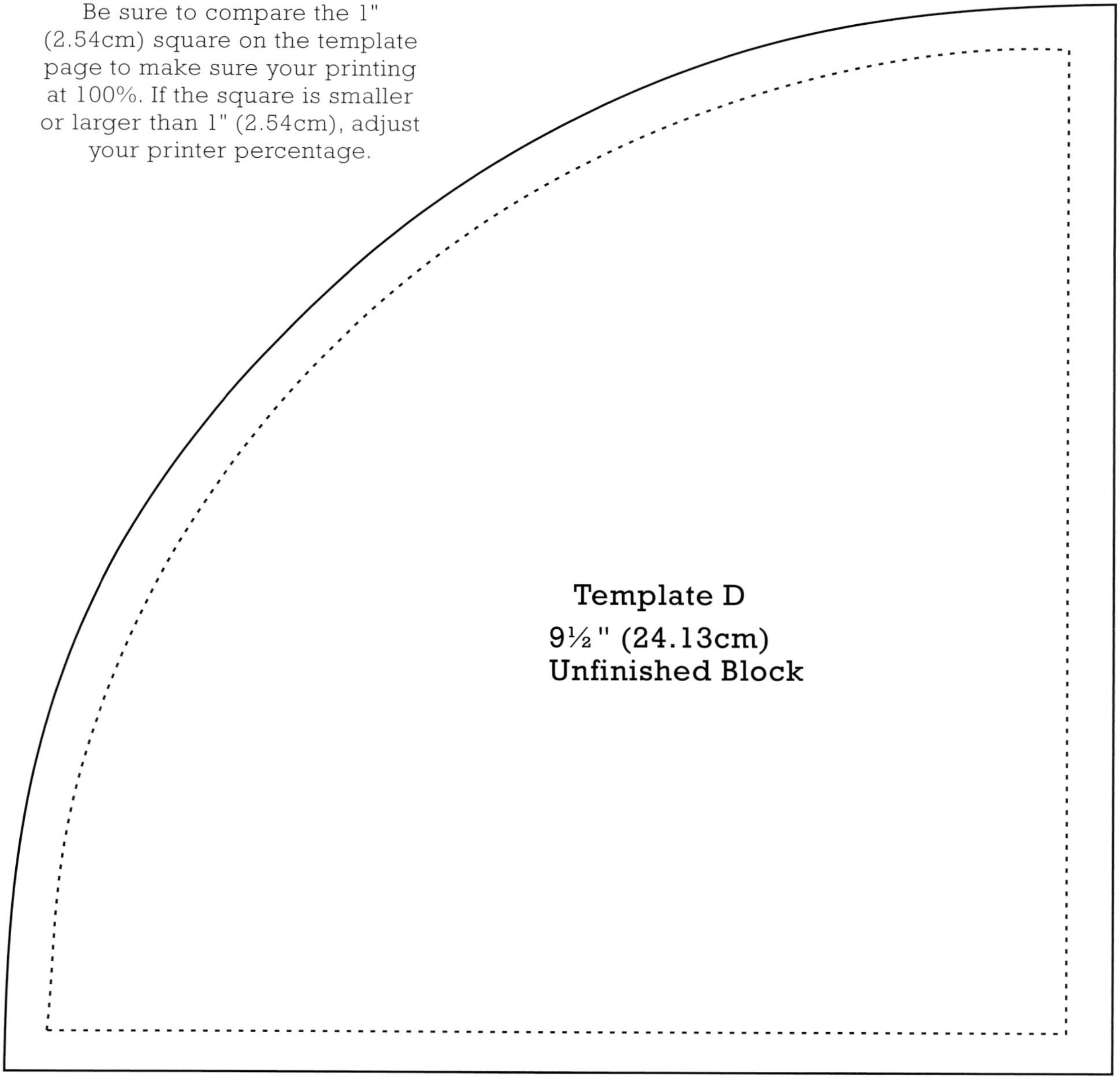

**Template D**
**9½" (24.13cm)**
**Unfinished Block**

# SHATTERED

This quilt started out with the traditional Darting Birds block. When I varied the size of the block within the quilt and played with color placement, a very dynamic design emerged.

So a quilt doesn't look too simple or uninteresting, consider pairing larger blocks with pairs of the same block in a smaller size as in this quilt.

## MODERN

Larger scale or intricate prints are a hallmark of recent fabric designs from many companies. Finding ways to use those prints in patchwork quilts without losing the overall impact of the fabric design can be a challenge.

One easy trick is to start by substantially increasing the scale of traditional blocks. Many quilt patterns focus on blocks that are 9–12" (22.86-30.48cm) in finished size. By exploring larger sizes, from 16–24" (40.64-60.96cm), the block patches are much larger so more of the focus is on the actual fabric design.

## TRADITIONAL

The Darting Birds blocks produces a very predictable quilt when blocks are set in a traditional setting. When it's set together, side by side, it creates a very dense quilt.

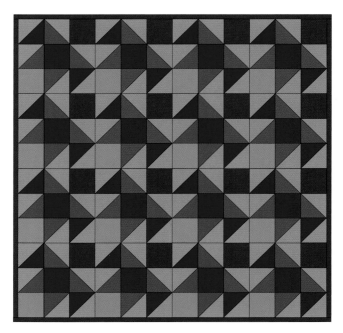

## LEAP OF FAITH

- Enlarging traditional blocks beyond the common 12" (30.48cm) finished size creates the perfect opportunity to showcase busy or larger-scale prints. Start with a favorite block, and then experiment with enlarging it and pairing it with multiples of a smaller size. Interesting intersections and design elements will emerge.

## COLOR LESSON

- Shattered uses an analogous color scheme—three colors that are close together on the color wheel—yellow, green and blue. By selecting a palette of colors that are near each other on the color wheel, you increase your odds of creating a visually appealing quilt.

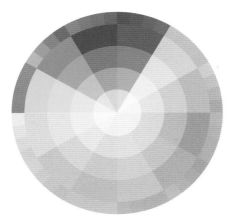

## MATERIALS

- 2½ yards (228.6cm) multi-colored print, Fabric 1, for sashing
- 2½ yards (228.6cm) gold print, Fabric 2, for blocks
- 1 yard (91.44 cm) dark gold, Fabric 3, for blocks
- ⅝ yard (57.15 cm) turquoise, Fabric 4, for blocks
- ⅞ yard (80.01cm) small-scale multi-print, Fabric 5, for blocks
- ⅞ yard (80.01cm) small-scale dark green print, Fabric 6, for blocks
- 1½ yards (137.16cm) dark green print, Fabric 7, for blocks
- 8 yards (731.52cm) backing
- ⅝ yard (57.15cm) binding

## CUTTING

BLOCK 1 (MAKE 4)

**From gold print (Fabric 2), cut:**
(2)  4⅜" (11.11cm) x WOF strips. From the strips cut: (12) 4⅜" (11.11cm) squares. Cut in half diagonally to make (24) Piece A triangles.

**From the turquoise print (Fabric 4), cut:**
(1)  4" (10.16cm) x WOF strip. From the strip cut: (8) 4" (10.16cm) B squares

**From the small-scale multi-print (Fabric 5), cut:**
(2)  4⅜" (11.11cm) x WOF strips. From the strips cut: (8) 4⅜" (11.11cm) squares. Cut in half diagonally to make (16) Piece A triangles.

**From the dark green small-scale print (Fabric 6), cut:**
(1)  4⅜" (11.11cm) x WOF strip. From the strip cut: (4) 4⅜" (11.11cm). Cut in half diagonally to make (8) Piece A triangles.
(1) 4" (10.16cm) x WOF strip. From the strip, cut: (4) 4" (10.16cm) B squares

## PIECING BLOCK 1 (MAKE 4)

1. Pair a gold print Fabric 2 triangle with a multi-print Fabric 5 triangle, right sides together. Sew with a ¼" (0.64cm) seam allowance along the long edge of the triangle. Press the seam toward the print. Repeat to make (16 ) pieced half-square triangle units.

**Make 16**

2. Repeat step 1 with a gold print Fabric 2 triangle and a dark green print Fabric 6 triangle. Make (8) pieced half-square triangle units.

**Make 8**

3. Lay out (2) turquoise Fabric 4 squares, a Fabric 6 square, and the half-square triangles from steps 1–2, as shown. Sew the block together in rows and sew the rows together to finish Block 1. Make (4) 11" (27.94cm) unfinished blocks.

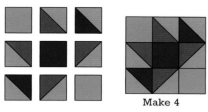
**Make 4**

## CUTTING BLOCK 2

### From the gold print (Fabric 2), cut:
(3) 4⅜" (11.11cm) x WOF strips.
  From the strips cut:
  (24) 4⅜" (11.11cm) squares. Cut in half diagonally to make (48) Piece A triangles.

### From the turquoise print (Fabric 4), cut:
(1) 4" (10.16cm) x WOF strip. From the strip cut:
  (8) 4" (10.16cm) B squares

### From the small-scale multi-print (Fabric 5), cut:
(2) 4⅜" (11.11cm) x WOF strips.
  From the strips cut:
(16) 4⅜" (11.11cm) squares. Cut in half diagonally to make (32) Piece A triangles.

### From the dark green small-scale print (Fabric 6), cut: (2) 4⅜" (11.11cm) x WOF strips.
### From the strips cut:
(16) 4⅜" (11.11cm) squares. Cut in half diagonally to make (32) Piece A triangles.
(1) 4" (10.16cm) x WOF strip. From the strip cut:
  (8) 4" (10.16cm) Piece B squares

### From the dark green print (Fabric 7), cut:
(1) 4" (10.16cm) x WOF strip. From the strip cut:
  (8) 4" (10.16cm) Piece B squares

## PIECING BLOCK 2 (MAKE 8)

1. Piece Block 2, following the illustration below.

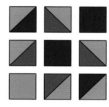

2. Lay out (1) turquoise Fabric 4 square, a Fabric 6 square, and the half-square triangles, as shown. Sew the block together in rows and sew the rows together to finish Block 2. Make (8).

**Make 8**

## CUTTING BLOCK 3

### From the gold print (Fabric 2), cut:
(2) 7⅞" (20.0cm) x WOF strips.
  From the strips, cut:
  (6) 7⅞" (20.0cm) squares. Cut in half diagonally to make (12) Piece C triangles. Cut the remaining strip into (4) 7½" (19.05cm) Piece D squares.

### From the small-scale multi-print (Fabric 5), cut:
(1) 7⅞" (20.0cm) x WOF strip.
  From the strip, cut:
  (4) 7⅞" (20.0cm) squares. Cut in half diagonally to make (8) Piece C triangles.

### From the dark green small-scale print (Fabric 6), cut:
(1) 7⅞" (20.0cm) x WOF strip.
  From the strip, cut:
  (2) 7⅞" (20.0cm) squares. Cut in half diagonally to make (4) Piece C triangles. Cut the remaining strip into (4) 7½" (19.05cm) Piece D squares.

## FEARLESS TAKEAWAYS

- When you're stumped on how to use a favorite "busy" print that is just too perfect to cut up in to tiny pieces, pick your favorite block and enlarge it to 18" (45.72cm) or beyond. Let the fabric do the work.

## CONFIDENCE BOOSTER

- If you're not sure how to enlarge a block, start with your basic block size and multiply by two. Then you will know that two of the smaller blocks will easily next to a larger block. Once you're confident with that math, you can move on to other variations of block sizes.

## PIECING BLOCK 3 (MAKE 2)

1. Piece Block 3, following the illustration below.

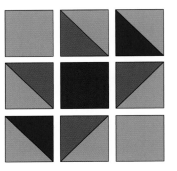

2. Lay out a dark green Fabric 6 square, (2) gold Fabric 2 squares and the half-square triangles, as shown. Sew the block together in rows and sew the rows together to finish Block 3. Make (2) 21½" (53.34cm) unfinished squares.

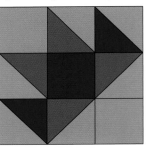

## CUTTING BLOCK 4

**From the gold print (Fabric 2), cut:**

(2)  7⅞" (20.0cm) x WOF strips.
     From the strips, cut:
     (6) 7⅞" (20.0cm) squares. Cut in half diagonally to make (12) Piece C triangles. Cut the remaining strip into (4) 7½" (19.05cm) Piece D squares.

**From the small-scale multi-print (Fabric 5), cut:**

(1)  7⅞" (20.0cm) x WOF strip. From the strip, cut:
     (4) 7⅞" (20.0cm) squares. Cut in half diagonally to make (8) Piece C triangles.
(2)  7½" x 14½" (19.05 x 36.83cm) rectangles
(2)  7½" x 21½" (19.05 x 54.61cm) rectangles

**From the dark green small-scale print (Fabric 6), cut:**

(1)  7⅞" (20.0cm) x WOF strip. From the strip, cut:
     (2) 7⅞" (20.0cm) squares. Cut in half diagonally to make (4) Piece C triangles. Cut the remaining strip into (4) 7½" (19.05cm) Piece D squares.

**From the multi-colored print (Fabric 1), cut:**

(1)  7½" (19.05cm) x WOF. From the strip, cut:
     (1) 7 ½" (19.05cm) square

## PIECING BLOCK 4 (MAKE 2)

1. Piece Block 4, following the illustration below.

2. Lay out (1) Fabric 6 square, (1) Fabric 1 square and the half-square triangles, as shown. Sew the block together in rows and sew the rows together.

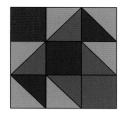

3. Sew (1) 7½" x 14" (19.05 x 36.83cm) rectangle to the right side of the block, and (1) 7½" x 21½" (19.05 x 54.61cm) rectangle to the bottom of Block 4. Make (2) blocks.

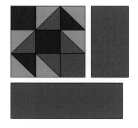 

**Make 2**

## CUTTING BLOCK 5

**From the dark gold print (Fabric 3), cut:**

(2) 7⅞" (20.0cm) x WOF strips.
From, the strips, cut:
(6) 7⅞" (20.0cm) squares. Cut in half diagonally to make (12) Piece C triangles. Cut the remaining strip into (4) 7½" (19.05cm) Piece D squares.

**From the turquoise print (Fabric 4), cut:**

(1) 7⅞" (20.0cm) x WOF strip. From the strip, cut:
(2) 7⅞" (20.0cm) squares. Cut in half diagonally to make (4) Piece C triangles.

**From the dark green print (Fabric 7), cut:**

(1) 7½" (19.05cm) x WOF. From the strip, cut:
(2) 7½" (19.05cm) Piece D squares

## PIECING BLOCK 5 (MAKE 2)

1. Piece Block 5, following the illustration below.

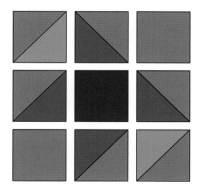

2. Lay out (1) Fabric 7 square, (2) dark gold Fabric 3 squares and the half-square triangles, as shown. Sew the block together in rows and sew the rows together to finish Block 5. Make (2) 21½" (53.34cm) unfinished squares.

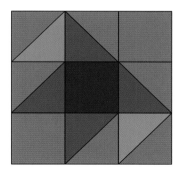

## CUTTING BLOCK 6

**From the dark gold print (Fabric 3), cut:**

(2) 7⅞" (20.0cm) x WOF strips. From the strips, cut:
(6) 7⅞" (20.0cm) squares. Cut in half diagonally to make (12) Piece C triangles. Cut the remaining strip into (4) 7½" (19.05cm) Piece D squares.

**From the small-scale multi-print (Fabric 5), cut:**

(1) 7⅞" (20.0cm) x WOF strip. From the strip, cut:
(4) 7⅞" (20.0cm) squares. Cut in half diagonally to make 8 Piece C triangles.

**From the turquoise print (Fabric 4), cut:**

(1) 7½" (19.05cm) x WOF. From the strip, cut:
(2) 7½" (19.05cm) Piece D squares

## PIECING BLOCK 6 (MAKE 2)

1. Piece Block 6, following the illustration below.

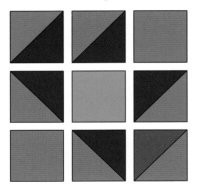

2. Lay out (1) Fabric 4 square, (2) dark gold Fabric
   3 squares and the half-square triangles, as shown.
   Sew the block together in rows and sew the rows
   together to finish Block 6. Make (2) 21½" (53.34cm)
   unfinished squares.

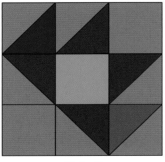

**Make 2**

## CUTTING FILLER BLOCKS AND SASHING

**From dark gold (Fabric 3), cut:**
(4)   14½" (36.83cm) Block A squares
(4)   4" X 7½" (10.16 x 19.05cm) Block B rectangles
(4)   4" x 11" (10.16 x 27.94cm) Block B rectangles

**From the multi-colored print (Fabric 1), cut:**
(4)   7½" (19.05cm) Block A squares
(6)   7½" x 21½" (19.05 x 54.61cm) Block A rectangles
(6)   7½" x 14½" (19.05 x 36.83cm) Block A rectangles

**Block B, 7½" (19.05cm)**

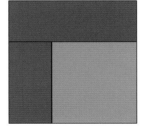

**Block A, 14½" (36.83cm)**

## QUILT ASSEMBLY

1. Referring to the Quilt Assembly Diagram, lay out the quilt blocks, as shown, paying attention to placement and orientation. Sew multiple unit blocks together first.

2. Sew the blocks together in rows and sew the rows together to finish the quilt top. It should measure 84½" (214.63cm) unfinished.

## FINISHING THE QUILT

1. Trim the selvedges and piece the backing yardage, using a ½" (1.27cm) seam.

2. Layer the quilt top, backing and batting. Quilt as desired.

3. Trim the selvedge from each of the (9) binding strips. Sew together using diagonal seams to make one long strip. Press the seams open. Fold the binding in half, wrong sides together, and press along the entire length of the strip. Attach the binding using your preferred method.

**SHATTERED**
Finished size: 84" (213.36cm)

# ABOUT THE AUTHOR

Sarah's love of quilting stems from her college days, when her mom sent her a pink dogwood quilt to grace the bed in her first apartment. The quilt was a comforting reminder of her home in the Lake of the Ozarks, where the dogwood blossoms always signaled the start of spring.

A few years later, married and expecting her first child, Sarah caught the nesting bug. Inspired by the treasured dogwood quilt, she bought a beginner's quilt book and crafted her first quilt. She continued to improve her skills through classes at local quilt guilds, as well as learning from gifted teachers throughout the United States. She has fully taking advantage of modern conveniences, such as rotary cutting and computer design, as they became available.

Today, Sarah is a fabric and pattern designer for Studio 37 Fabrics, a division of Marcus Fabrics, with countless quilts to her credit. Her work has been featured regularly in both *McCall's Quilting* and *McCall's Quick Quilts* for the past several years. Additionally, Sarah's quilts have appeared in *Make Modern, Simply Moderne, American Patchwork & Quilting* and *Quilts & More*, as well as many other magazines. She is also the author of *Morse Code Quilts*, Landauer Publishing/Fox Chapel Publishing.